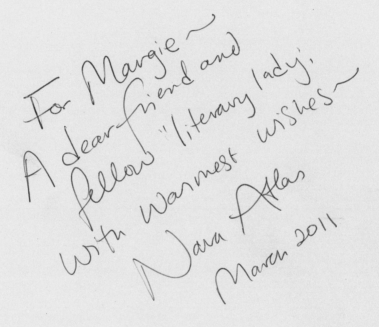

For Margie~
A dear friend and
fellow "literary lady",
with warmest wishes~
Nava Atlas
March 2011

The *Literary Ladies'*
GUIDE TO THE WRITING LIFE

Alcott   Austen   Brontë   Cather   Ferber   L'Engle

Montgomery   Nin   Sand   Stowe   Wharton   Woolf

The *Literary Ladies'*
GUIDE TO THE WRITING LIFE

Inspiration and Advice from
Celebrated Women Authors
Who Paved the Way

BY NAVA ATLAS

SELLERS
PUBLISHING

Published by Sellers Publishing, Inc.
Copyright © 2011 Nava Atlas

All rights reserved.

Page design by Nava Atlas and Amy Papaelias

Sellers Publishing, Inc.
161 John Roberts Road, South Portland, Maine 04106
Visit our Web site: www.sellerspublishing.com • E-mail: rsp@rsvp.com

ISBN 13: 978-1-4162-0632-3
Library of Congress Control Number: 2010933894

10 9 8 7 6 5 4 3 2 1

Printed in China.

Contents

Prologue 7

Introduction 11

Chapter One: **Becoming a Writer** 19

Chapter Two: **Developing a Voice** 37

Chapter Three: **Tools of the Trade** 57

Chapter Four: **Conquering Inner Demons** 73

Chapter Five: **The Writer Mother** 91

Chapter Six: **Rejection and Acceptance** 109

Chapter Seven: **Money Matters** 135

Chapter Eight: **Farther Along the Path** 153

Sources, Notes, and Acknowledgments 177

In memory of my mother,
who loved to write —
and who would have read
this book with pride

Prologue

The author at age five, posing for her first publicity portrait

I can scarcely remember a time when I didn't love writing. Even as a small child, I was rarely without a pencil in my hand, with which I wrote and drew in equal measure — that is, when my nose wasn't in a book. When it came time to decide what to study, visual art won out, even though the first thing I did after high school was to write a novella. It featured a gifted yet obnoxious eight-year-old named Phillippe, who runs away from his uncle's posh French Riviera home to become a drug dealer in Marseilles, and shortly thereafter, the star acrobat of a Turkish circus. At the time, I deemed it clever and hilarious, but I have no doubt it was dreadful.

Even as an art student in college, words were my constant companions; in my spare time I devoured the major Russian novels and other tomes by Thomas Mann and Marcel Proust (I haven't had patience for such hefty literature since). I was also a prolific letter-writer and often kept a journal. My artwork was nearly always embellished with text; my writing often included images. It seemed a natural segue to apply my skills to illustrate and design books as a way to make a living. That's exactly what I did, striking out as a freelancer in New York City, doing jobs for publishers — mainly interior illustrations and cover designs; nothing brilliant, merely the means to pay rent.

A highlight of this bohemian existence included a whirlwind romance, followed by marriage, to a fellow starving artist. My new husband was particularly enthused about the vegetarian meals I made on our limited budget, and urged me to write down the recipes I concocted. Before long, I hatched the idea to create an unusual cookbook. Applying my literature-geek sensibility to the project, I teamed my recipes and illustrations with food-related quotes by the likes of Mark Twain, William Shakespeare, George Bernard Shaw, and other renowned authors (oddly, scarcely a woman was to be found among them). Still in my twenties when *Vegetariana* was published, its modest yet solid success set me on a path I never expected — that of a cookbook author and food writer.

With this steady "day job" of cookbook and food-article writing, I pursued my parallel path in the arts. I also attempted to write two novels, doing tons of research and lots of drafts for each, but when the going got tough, I gave up. If I'd known more about how writers experienced the creative process, I would have been prepared for the fact that the path is often arduous — especially for long, sustained works. I thought I lacked ability when writing felt hard, but what was missing was insight and perseverance. Once my sons were born, it was easy to say that I had neither the time nor patience for working on a novel or pursuing serious art exhibits. This attitude also explains the fifteen-year gap in my art resumé. I did what seemed easier to accomplish (mainly the food writing) during the years of juggling work and family.

I don't see fiction as somehow more noble than nonfiction — neither the writing nor the reading of it. I admire any kind of writing that's thoughtful and well-crafted. I've always loved to cook and believe in the ideals of a plant-based lifestyle, so I've never regretted the years I've devoted to writing about healthy food. All that, plus a couple of published humor books, has added up to a gratifying and rewarding career, one that was nearly ideal in allowing me to devote my energies to raising a family as well. But if you're like me, you get to a certain point in your life and say, "Wait — wasn't I supposed to do X and Y by this age?" In my case, X was doing weightier forms of writing, and Y was gaining more of a foothold in the visual arts field.

Once my sons were in their teens, I had the notion to go to graduate school. And since I was still more of an art student than an academic type (despite my bookishness), I entered a program to bring my rusty skills in design and digital processes up to speed. I also wanted to learn how to make limited-edition artist's books, a form of expression that's perfect for marrying my dual penchant for words and images. In fact, the idea for this book was born in one of my book arts courses. My interests in the creative process, literature, and gender issues all converged as I started collecting first-person narratives by well-known women authors on their writing lives. Though the original, diminutive version (of which I made three very badly hand-bound copies) was also titled *The Literary Ladies' Guide to the Writing Life,* it looked completely different from the finished book you're reading now.

After the requisite few years of languishing in a drawer, a day trip to The Mount (Edith Wharton's home in the Berkshires) reinvigorated my interest in the concept. First, I created a blog called Dear Literary Ladies, followed by the proposal for this book, which underwent a colorful makeover on its way to publication in its present form. With the learning curve in action, I've been able to use my updated (that is, digital) design skills as the co-designer of this book, along with being its author. That's what's fascinating about the creative process: sometimes ideas need their own time and rhythm to unfold, yet other times you must consciously push to make them blossom. Often, it's a combination of both, as has been the case with this book and its related projects.

Having completed this book, I know that when (not if, but when) I try my hand again at a long, complex narrative, I'll be better prepared. Now I have a better sense of what the creative process of accomplished writers looks like, and I'm able to imagine what it feels like, too. Learning about the writing lives of these authors has been comforting, illuminating, and above all, inspiring. Given the nutshell history I've related, it may not be surprising that I have my sights set on creating a graphic novel in the near future. I can hardly wait to start writing and drawing on the same page again. Wish me luck! And I wish the readers of *The Literary Ladies' Guide to the Writing Life* the same in your literary and creative pursuits.

Introduction

WHAT'S BEHIND THE UNIVERSAL YEARNING TO SET THOUGHTS TO paper, despite the arduous process and uncertain results? And why is that solitary figure at a desk with a quill, a pen, a typewriter, or these days, a computer, the object of such ongoing fascination and desire? Edna Ferber believed that "the writer is a writer because [she] cannot help it. It is a compulsion. Sometimes it is called a gift, but actually it is an urge for expression that simply cannot be denied." George Sand called writing "an indestructible passion" and Anaïs Nin regarded it as essential as breathing.

Throughout this book, the twelve classic authors I refer to as Literary Ladies will guide us through all aspects of the writing life. My comments are here to connect writing lives past to those experienced in the present by the likes of you and me. You'll be amazed by how much you have in common with Edith Wharton (who struggled to feel worthy of success), Louisa May Alcott (who badly needed money), Madeleine L'Engle (who could have papered an entire house with her rejection letters), and other writers in this book.

With their legacies cemented, and many works perennially in print, it's easy to imagine that classic authors burst into literary glory fully formed. Not true! Few practiced their art under ideal conditions. Some, like Harriet Beecher Stowe and Louisa May Alcott, were driven to the pen by financial need. Others, like Jane Austen and Charlotte Brontë, captured the human condition despite limited formal education and narrow life experience. Still others (like Virginia Woolf and L.M. Montgomery) persisted in their pursuit while grappling with mood disorders. They may have cried into their journals or lamented in letters, but in all my delving into their private thoughts and creative processes, I rarely encountered anything resembling excuses. Whether or not in tandem with the rare unshakable confidence of Willa Cather, each author possessed, at least inwardly, a fierce drive and determination to succeed.

To arrive at this group of a dozen authors, I pored through letters, journals, memoirs, and interviews and chose those who had a great deal to say about the creative, practical, and emotional components of the writing life. I wanted to focus on writers who are deceased, since being a successful woman in the arts was more challenging in the past. We'll journey from the life of Jane Austen (who was born in the late 1700s) through that of Madeleine L'Engle (who was the only author in this group to live into the 21st century). There were other authors I would have loved to include, such as Mary Wollstonecraft Shelley (author of Frankenstein) and George Eliot (like George Sand, Mary Ann Evans took the male pseudonym to ensure that her works were taken seriously). But I didn't find enough in their letters and journals on their writing lives. Nor was it feasible to include, though I dearly wanted to, at least one African-American author from the past. Imagine the odds against success for a white woman in the nineteenth century and multiply that a thousandfold for any female of color. In the twentieth century, a very small number of black women writers broke the barrier before the Civil Rights era, and one true pioneer was Zora Neale Hurston. In the 1920s, she was the only black student at Barnard College, and became a member of the Harlem Renaissance literary movement. But despite a brilliant start, her life became a cautionary tale. Though Hurston did write fascinating autogiographical narratives, I couldn't find sufficient material on her writing life to make her one of the Literary Ladies.

In following the writing lives of the Literary Ladies, what you'll find are not instructions on the how-to of writing (which look remarkably similar from one writing manual to another) but something that might prove even more valuable — a treasury of intimate glimpses into the unfolding creative process across twelve brilliant careers. I can think of no better mentors and muses for the journey than the classic women authors we'll get to know in the pages ahead, starting with the following introduction to each of their unique stories.

Louisa May Alcott (1832–1888) conducted her career as a professional determined to profit from her pen. Financial need stoked her drive as she became the primary breadwinner in her family at a young age. She credited hard work rather than talent for her success. Though Alcott claimed that her greatest reward was the esteem of the "young folks" who were her readers, she was never modest in her demands to be paid what she felt she was worth, and lived to see her work earn a fortune. Major works: *Little Women, Jo's Boys, Little Men, Rose in Bloom, Eight Cousins, Hospital Sketches, An Old-Fashioned Girl.*

Jane Austen's (1775–1817) writing life was that of the inimitable artist — behind her charm and modesty she continually hints that she was in full mastery of her gift and cared deeply about getting published despite myths to the contrary. Though only a small portion of her letters survive, I couldn't imagine not including her in this collection; fortunately, ther's enough material in her first-person narratives to reveal a sense of the woman behind the pen. She sought to create perfection and grace, no matter what the outcome. Major works: *Pride and Prejudice, Sense and Sensibility, Emma, Mansfield Park, Northanger Abbey, Persuasion.*

Charlotte Brontë's (1816–1855) life as a writer was romantic as well as tragic. She lived to tell the tale of how she and her two sisters took masculine pseudonyms to improve their chances of finding publishers, and the challenges and prejudices they faced in their pursuits. Her brother and two literary sisters, Emily and Anne, died tragically young of illness when barely out of their twenties; she herself died just shy of age thirty-nine from complications due to pregnancy (her first). Her story is one of sheer genius meeting tireless determination. Some of her contemporaries said of Charlotte that she would have traded her genius for beauty. I don't believe it; do you? Major works: *Jane Eyre, Shirley, Villette, The Professor.*

Willa Cather (1873–1947) created a body of work that represented consummate craftsmanship of the written word. Her novels, known for their stark beauty and spare language, reflect her philosophy that writing is an art as well as a skill that can be honed and polished. Cather's considerable wisdom has been fully preserved, especially in the numerous interviews she granted despite her professed disdain for the press and fame in general. Major works: *My Ántonia, O Pioneers!, Death Comes for the Archbishop, Alexander's Bridge, Song of the Lark.*

Edna Ferber (1885–1968) is a name perhaps less known today than some of the others in this group, but she was considered one of the most successful authors of the mid-twentieth century. With their strong female characters, panoramic plots filled with travel and adventure, and colorful locales, most of her novels became not only bestsellers but Academy Award-winning movies. Her theme is the complete and utter devotion to the writing life, almost to the exclusion of all else. Major works: *So Big, Giant, Cimarron, Saratoga Trunk, Show Boat.*

Madeleine L'Engle's (1918–2007) writing life can best be described as one of sheer perseverance. Best known for her award-winning young adult science fiction, L'Engle recorded in detail the long years during which her work was rejected as "too dark and difficult for children." Hers is a story of triumph following years of silence and frustration. She persisted because she felt compelled to, and was finally rewarded not just with sales but also more than a dozen honorary degrees and numerous other awards. She also exemplified the working artist who was an involved parent. Major works: *A Wrinkle in Time, A Wind in the Door, A Swiftly Tilting Planet, Meet the Austins, The Arm of the Starfish.*

L.M. Montgomery (1874–1942) produced one of the sunniest characters in children's literature, Anne Shirley of *Anne of Green Gables,* while her own life was filled with cares, including nearly lifelong depression. Her stories' blend of nostalgia and realism have captivated readers for generations. Lucy Maud Montgomery kept copious journals, and the theme that emerges from her reflections was that despite her personal troubles, she viewed her writing as a vehicle for bringing joy to others. Major works: *Anne of Green Gables* (series), *Emily of New Moon* (series), *The Story Girl, A Tangled Web.*

Anaïs Nin (1903–1977) experienced the practice of writing as a grand passion and a path to delving deeply into the self. In this sense, Nin foreshadowed the immediacy of today's world of self-revelatory memoir and blogging. Best known for her multi-volume *Diary* series, which became a touchstone of feminist thought, she also broke ground as a writer of female erotica, and was a splendid essayist as well. Major works: *The Early Diary of Anaïs Nin* (four volumes), *The Diary of Anaïs Nin* (seven volumes), *Delta of Venus, Little Birds, In Favor of the Sensitive Man and Other Essays.*

George Sand (1804–1876) embodied a capacity for prodigious output and passionate living, with a penchant for drama in her everyday life (not the least of which were her countless romantic entanglements). With literally scores of novels to her credit, she also wrote several plays and countless shorter works. It would be nearly impossible for any contemporary woman to emulate such an existence (and even the thought of doing so is exhausting), but she remains a model for creating a full palette of love, productivity, and family. Major works: *Indiana, Mauprat, Consuelo, Le Petite Fadette, Lélia, La Mare au Diable.*

Harriet Beecher Stowe (1811–1896) was the ultimate working mother, obliged to supplement her husband's meager income to support their large family. Stowe's overarching theme as a writer is that of one who consciously used storytelling as a catalyst for change. Though she bore seven children and struggled in genteel poverty, she found a way to write for profit and purpose. Though the literary merits of her work have long been debated, there is little dispute that *Uncle Tom's Cabin*  caused a major shift in public perception of slavery. Major Works: *Uncle Tom's Cabin, Dred, The Minister's Wooing, Old Town Folks.*

Edith Wharton (1862–1937) typified the *grande dame* of American letters; everything about her, from her wealthy background to her stately demeanor, suggested a woman in possession of herself. However, beneath the surface was a deep insecurity about her talent and abilities, one she gradually overcame. Her impressive and respected body of fiction and nonfiction was crowned with a Pulitzer Prize and other honors. Major works: *The House of Mirth, The Age of Innocence, Ethan Frome, The Custom of the Country, The Valley of Decision, The Reef.*

Virginia Woolf (1882–1941) epitomized rare literary genius, producing a body of work, both fiction and nonfiction, considered among the most groundbreaking in twentieth-century literature. Nurtured by husband Leonard Woolf and beloved by the literary circle of her Bloomsbury colleagues, Woolf might have lived the ideal writing life were it not for her mental breakdowns. Her diaries, letters, and essays provide insightful illumination of the writing life. Major works: *The Years, Jacob's Room, To the Lighthouse, Mrs. Dalloway, Orlando, A Room of One's Own.*

Through the narratives in this book, we get a glimpse of so much that is universal in the writing life, yet at the same time, it becomes apparent that there are few hard and fast rules: Louisa May Alcott responded to her readers' letters asking for writing advice with variations on "One person's method is no rule for another. Each must work in [her] own way, and the only drill needed is to keep writing, and profit by criticism." Advice and observations flow from the Literary Ladies' pens, and though much of it is applicable to men as well as women who write, it's particularly resonant with the female experience. To that end, please note that I've converted the default gender of *he* when used in the narratives to *she*, which will appear in brackets. Tiny edits have been made to punctuation and the like, to keep the grammatical style of this book consistent, but otherwise, the authors' voices have been left intact — even when they used embellished language, like "explosional" and "remaineth."

From the time Aphra Behn (1640–1689) established herself as the first professional author in the English language, through the present time, it has become incrementally easier for women to write for self-expression and pleasure. It has also become completely acceptable to write for profit and glory without hiding behind masculine pseudonyms as Charlotte Brontë (Currer Bell) and Aurore Dupin (George Sand) did. However, it's still challenging to find the focus to write while raising children, to get that first work published, to make a living by writing, and above all, to have the courage to send one's words out into the world. It's still painful to face rejection, daunting to experience writer's block, and difficult to accept that self-doubt is part of the creative process.

In the introduction to *The Writer on Her Work,* a collection of essays by contemporary women authors, editor Janet Sternburg aptly states, "A woman writer in the future may well feel released from the questions of gender and its effects on her work, but I believe the experience of her predecessors will be telling." Today, we can look back at the efforts of these Literary Ladies with gratitude, knowing they paved the way for all women who follow their paths.

CHAPTER ONE | *Becoming a Writer*

I believe I could never exhaust
the supply of material lying
within me. The deeper I plunge,
the more I discover. There is
no bottom to my heart and no
limit to the acrobatic feats of my
imagination.

— Anaïs Nin
The Early Diaries of Anaïs Nin,
entry dated October, 1921

"WHY WRITE?" IS A UNIVERSAL QUESTION WITHOUT A SIMPLE ANSWER. Though it will be directly addressed by some of the Literary Ladies in the pages of this chapter, the exploration of the writing impulse is what unites all the subjects explored throughout this book.

For some, writing is about connection and the sharing of stories that illuminate aspects of the human condition. For others, it's a compulsion, something you do because you honestly can't help yourself. And for others still, it's a way to surmount obstacles. You'll see all those "whys" reflected in the musings that follow. When Anaïs Nin examined the "why" of writing, it wasn't for money, fame, or glory. Rather, it filled a need as elemental as breathing, and that's what worked for her. It may be what works for you — or not. Louisa May Alcott's answer may have been less existential and more practical, along the lines of "Because it's a profession that can pay a determined woman very well, when few others do." The Literary Ladies are here to illuminate some of the distinct possibilities. Fortunately, there's more than one answer to "why write?"

When asked why she wrote, Flannery O'Connor may have been flippant when she replied, "Because I'm good at it." Or perhaps her answer was forthright and true. You become good at what you focus on and engage in most. Longing to write without the attendant practice never made anyone a writer. Knowing why you write helps, as does learning how others did it — especially those who succeeded so brilliantly.

GEORGE SAND: OF PASSION AND PURPOSE

 I am more than ever intent upon following a literary career. In spite of the repugnance which I sometimes experience, despite the days of idleness and fatigue which cause me to break off my work, in spite of the life, more than quiet, which I lead here, I feel that henceforth my existence has an aim. I have a purpose in view, a task before me, and, if I may use the word, a passion. For the profession of writing is nothing else but a violent, indestructible passion. When it has once entered people's heads it never leaves them.

— From a letter to a friend (Jules Boucoiran),
  March, 1831

MANY OF US WHO SCRATCH OUT SENTENCES AND paragraphs that we hope to turn into publishable prose have paused to ponder the "why" of writing. When it goes well, it can be as consuming as a passionate love affair. But when the going gets tough, or when self-doubt creeps in, "why" can become "what's the point?" Zora Neale Hurston (1891–1960) wisely advised: "Perhaps it is just as well to be rash and foolish for a while. If writers were too wise, perhaps no books would be written at all. It might be better to ask yourself 'Why' afterwards than before ... There is no agony like bearing an untold story inside you."

George Sand is one of the most colorful literary figures of all time. Born in Paris in 1804 as Amantine Aurore Lucile Dupin, she remains one of France's best-known authors. Are you ready for this literary laundry list? Some sources credit her for having written about seventy novels, others, eighty; even thirty would have been amazing, considering that she also wrote massive numbers of short stories, essays, journalistic pieces, plays, and a multi-volume autobiography. Of her fiction, her first novel, *Indiana* (1832), along with *Lélia* (1833), and *Mauprat* (1837) are the most enduring. Though her outsized biography and persona are perhaps better known in the English-speaking world, her work was much admired by many of her literary contemporaries. It was, however, considered unseemly and completely unfeminine by others.

On the following page, three authors weigh in on an essential question relating to the "why" of writing: for whom are you doing it? Is it to shine a light for others, or for your own satisfaction? Or is it neither — do you write because you are meant to do so, and it feels as if you have no other choice? All three views are represented here. Writers are indeed a complicated bunch. Join the club!

George Sand: To enlighten others

One writes for all the world, for all who need to be initiated; when one is not understood, one is resigned and recommences. When one is understood, one rejoices and continues. There lies the whole secret of our persevering labors and of our love of art. What is art without the hearts and minds on which it pours? A sun which would not project rays and would give life to no one.

— From a letter to Gustave Flaubert, 1866

Edna Ferber: To please oneself

This is certain: I never have written a line except to please myself. I never have written with an eye to what is called the public or the market or the trend or the editor or the reviewer. Good or bad, popular or unpopular, lasting or ephemeral, the words I have put down on paper were the best words I could summon at the time to express the thing I wanted more than anything else to say.

— *A Peculiar Treasure*, 1939

No, you don't write for yourself or for others. You write out of a deep inner necessity. If you are a writer, you have to write, just as you have to breathe, or if you're a singer you have to sing. But you're not aware of doing it for someone. This need to write was for me as strong as the need to live. I needed to live, but I also needed to record what I lived. It was a second life, it was my way of living in a more heightened way.

— Anaïs Nin,
   "The Artist as Magician,"
   interview, 1973

JANE AUSTEN AND CHARLOTTE BRONTË MIGHT BE LINKED BY THEIR early nineteenth-century British backgrounds and legions of devotees, but, according to James Edward Austen-Leigh, nephew of the former, "No two writers could be more unlike each other than Jane Austen and Charlotte Brontë; so much so that the latter was unable to understand why the former was admired, and confessed that she herself 'should hardly like to live with her ladies and gentlemen, in their elegant but confined houses.'"

Born in 1775 in Hampshire, England, Jane Austen was part of a convivial middle-class family consisting of five brothers and an elder sister, Cassandra, with whom she was very close. The Austens valued education; the two girls briefly attended boarding school and continued to receive further education at home. Jane's talent was recognized early on, and the men in her family played key roles in getting her works published. Six exquisite novels — crafted with compassion, humor, and insight into the travails of the sexes and social classes — assured her lofty position in literary history.

Similarly, Charlotte Brontë, born in 1816 in a small Yorkshire village, was part of a clerical family that valued education for their daughters as well as their sons. All five of her siblings' lives were tragically short. She and her sisters Emily (whose masterwork, *Wuthering Heights,* is often considered a greater achievement than Charlotte's own *Jane Eyre*) and Anne (best known for *Agnes Grey*) formed a tight circle of literary endeavor and mutual support.

Both Austen and Brontë wrote profusely in their youths, cementing their literary aspirations early on (a good thing, considering their abbreviated life spans; Austen died at 42, Brontë at 38). According to Austen-Leigh, "Each writer equally resisted interference with her own natural style of composition." Though both Austen and Brontë resisted influence from anyone else's voice, both authors have aided countless others in finding theirs. Countless spin-offs, imitations (pale and otherwise), and homages to their work have been published, from Daphne du Maurier's *Jane Eyre*-inspired modern gothic, *Rebecca*, to Seth Grahame-Smith's bizarre mash-up, *Pride and Prejudice and Zombies*.

Separated by a generation, both authors lived in an era when writing, let alone publication, was a challenging (yet not unheard of) occupation for genteel women to pursue. Yet both possessed the inner conviction that they deserved to be heard.

Jane Austen: How she started to feel like a writer

 I begin already to weigh my words and sentences more than I did, and am looking about for a sentiment, an illustration or a metaphor in every corner of the room. Could my Ideas flow as fast as the rain in the Store closet it would be charming.

— From a letter to her sister, 1809

Charlotte Brontë:
Even she wrote query letters

Steventon, Jane Austen's birthplace

 It is evident that unknown authors have great difficulties to contend with, before they can succeed in bringing their works before the public. Can you give me any hint as to the way in which these difficulties are best met? For instance, in the present case, where a work of fiction is in question, in what form would a publisher be most likely to accept the MS., whether offered as a work of three vols., or as tales which might be published in numbers, or as contributions to a periodical?

What publishers would be most likely to receive favourably a proposal of this nature?

Would it suffice to write to a publisher on the subject, or would it be necessary to have recourse to a personal interview?

— From a letter to a prospective publisher, 1846

Village of Haworth, home of the Brontës

HARRIET BEECHER STOWE:
HOW A MOTHER AND ACTIVIST TOOK UP THE PEN

 I was married when I was twenty-five to a man rich in Greek and Hebrew and Latin and Arabic, and alas, rich in nothing else…But then I was abundantly furnished with wealth of another sort. I had two little curly headed twin daughters to begin with and my stock in this line has gradually increased until I have been the mother of seven children, the most beautiful and most loved of whom lies buried near my Cincinnati residence. It was at his dying bed and at his grave that I learned what a poor slave mother may feel when her child is torn away from her.

During long years of struggling with poverty and sickness, and a hot, debilitating climate, my children grew up around me. The nursery and the kitchen were my principal fields of labor. Some of my friends, pitying my trials, copied and sent a number of little sketches from my pen to certain liberally paying "Annuals" with my name. With the first money that I earned in this way I bought a feather-bed!

… After this I thought that I had discovered the philosopher's stone. So when a new carpet or mattress was going to be needed, or when, at the close of the year, it began to be evident that my family accounts "wouldn't add up," then I used to say to my faithful friend and factotum Anna, who shared all my joys and sorrows, "Now, if you will keep the babies and attend to the things in the house for one day, I'll write a piece, and then we shall be out of the scrape." So I became an author — very modest at first, I do assure you, and remonstrating very seriously with the friends who had thought it best to put my name to the pieces by way of getting up a reputation…

— From a letter to a fellow abolitionist (Eliza Cabot Follen), 1853

Like a number of other Literary Ladies,
Harriet Elisabeth Beecher grew up in a family of progressive thinkers. She was born in Litchfield, Connecticut in 1811, and though by no means wealthy, her family members included ministers, authors, and educators who were well known in their time. She showed an early talent for writing, starting her career in earnest in her early twenties by contributing articles to numerous publications. Having such a steadily paying profession came in handy, as around the same time she married a penniless clergyman, Calvin Stowe.

Compelled to supplement her husband's meager income to support their growing family (they had seven children, though one died very young), she did so by writing anything and everything she could sell. This included sketches, poems, religious tracts — whatever might bring in a few extra dollars. Living in Cincinnati from 1832 to 1850, the Stowes met escaped slaves from Kentucky and got to hear of their plights. This was the impetus for Harriet's desire to use her talent to give slavery a human face and expose its injustice. Her sister-in-law, Isabella Jones Beecher, urged her to harness this talent: "Now, Hattie, if I could use a pen as you can, I would write something that would make this whole nation feel what an accursed thing slavery is."

Raising so many children while needing to do paid writing made it a dream deferred, but *Uncle Tom's Cabin* was published at last in 1853 and became the bestselling novel of the nineteenth century (and the second bestselling book right after the Bible). Through memorable fictional characters, this self-described "little bit of a woman ... about as thin and dry as a pinch of snuff," managed to shift public perception of slavery at home and around the world.

*T*he way to be great lies through books, now, and not through battles.

— Harriet Beecher Stowe,
  The Pearl of Orr's Island, 1862

Louisa May Alcott regarded her writing life above all as a dignified, paying profession. Born in 1832, and having lived most of her life in Massachusetts (first Boston, then Concord), she learned the value of an honest day's work at an early age. In fact, had we an opportunity to ask whether she considered herself a workhorse or an *artiste*, I'm fairly confident she would have chosen the former. Financial need stoked her determination to profit from her pen, becoming the breadwinner in her family while still fairly young. She supplanted her hapless father, the dreamy philosopher Bronson Alcott, as the primary support of her beloved mother and sisters. Doing so became both a burden and a source of pride. She possessed a touch of the martyr, which some Alcott scholars believe caused her to downplay and undervalue her considerable talent.

It's wonderful when an author can voice her reason for writing — and indeed her reason for being — through her heroines. Even through the veil of fiction, it rings true. We know Alcott as the author of genteel fiction for girls (though she had another, very different literary side, as we'll soon discover). She was also an active abolitionist, and promoted suffrage and other rights for women. She used fiction as a means to promote her progressive philosophies to those whom she hoped would benefit most — girls and young women.

Through the spirited central character of *Rose in Bloom*, at right, Alcott voices her own ideals, including the need for reform in women's education, dress, and especially their right to work at chosen professions. For Alcott, that meant writing, of course, because it was the way a determined woman such as herself could make a comfortable living, rather than settle for the scant wages offered by most professions deemed suitable for women.

We've got minds and souls as well as hearts; ambition and talents as well as beauty and accomplishments; and we want to live and learn as well as love and be loved. I'm sick of being told that is all a woman is fit for! I won't have anything to do with love until I prove that I am something beside a housekeeper and a baby-tender!

— Louisa May Alcott
Rose in Bloom, 1876

NOT LONG AFTER L.M. MONTGOMERY'S BIRTH ON PRINCE EDWARD Island, Canada in 1874, her mother died and her father abandoned her, leaving her to be raised by her paternal grandparents. She shared her identity as an orphan with her most memorable fictional character, Anne Shirley of the *Anne of Green Gables* series. That she produced one of the sunniest characters in children's literature seems somewhat ironic in light of her accumulating woes, including a lifelong battle with depression.

Like many bright young women of her social milieu, Montgomery earned a teaching degree, and briefly taught before working as a proofreader and copy editor at the Halifax *Chronicle*. All the while, becoming a published author was her dearest ambition. She started by writing short stories and serialized fiction, undaunted by numerous rejections. Upon the first acceptance of a poem, she wrote in her journal: "The moment we see our first darling brain-child in black type is never to be forgotten." At age 21 she sold her first short story for five dollars, and never looked back.

Like Alcott, Montgomery held no lofty view of her own talent, though she savored her gift for storytelling and ability to earn good money doing what she loved. Hers was an exception to the prevailing view of writing as an arduous (and sometimes agonizing) process. It was her greatest joy, and an escape from the troubles that grew ever more tangled as she aged, not the least of which were a husband who suffered from mental illness and serious legal battles over her most lucrative literary properties. Despite her own ongoing struggles with depression and breakdowns, she truly believed that her reason for writing was simply to bring happiness to readers, even as it eluded her.

"I'd like to add some beauty to life," said Anne dreamily. "I don't exactly want to make people know more...though I know that is the noblest ambition...but I'd love to make them have a pleasanter time because of me...to have some little joy or happy thought that would never have existed if I hadn't been born."

— L.M Montgomery, from
Anne of Avonlea, 1909

Read Charlotte Brontë's life. A very interesting, but sad one. So full of talent; and after working long, just as success, love, and happiness come, she dies.

Wonder if I shall ever be famous for people to care to read my story and struggles. I can't be a C.B., but I may do a little something yet.

— Louisa May Alcott
From her journal,
entry dated June, 1857

LOUISA MAY ALCOTT LED A DOUBLE LIFE — AT least in literary terms. On the surface, she was Jo March, her alter ego among the sisters portrayed in her best-known and most autobiographical work, *Little Women*. What's less well-known and more surprising is that Alcott cranked out a large body of thrillers, gothics, and sensational tales under various pseudonyms, allowing her to support her family while searching for her literary voice. Contrary as they seemed to her own life and values, she seemed to take some perverse pleasure in dark themes, returning to them even after financial need no longer compelled her to do this sort of formula writing.

It's no surprise that as an aspiring writer, around age twenty-four, she admired Charlotte Brontë; the longing to gain recognition for her work was present despite the modest phrasing. While Brontë's gothic, *Jane Eyre*, became not only an instant bestseller but an enduring literary classic, Alcott's "sensation tales" as they were called, are largely forgotten. One of her novels, *A Long Fatal Love Chase*, pseudonymously written as A.M. Barnard, was actually republished in 1995 after the identity of its famed author was discovered. It's a typical gothic melodrama — and the title is so transparent! Obviously, the term "spoiler" had not been coined.

Willful as a child, and still so as a young woman, she seemed to dare herself, with a kind of "I'll show them" attitude, rejecting the more acceptable feminine profession of teaching that was practically handed to her. About her penchant for writing thrillers she wrote, "I hope it is good drill for fancy and language." Whether tossing off anonymous melodramas or recording personal experiences like the well-received *Hospital Sketches* (about her stint as a Civil War nurse), Alcott was single-minded in her pursuit of publication and never took no for an answer.

Louisa May Alcott: "I can write, and I'll prove it"

 January, 1862 — E.P. Peabody wanted me to open a
Kindergarten, and Mr. Barnard gave a room at the Warren Street
Chapel. Don't like to teach, but take what comes; so when Mr. F.
offered $40 to fit up with, twelve pupils, and his patronage, I began ...

May. — School finished for me, and I paid Miss N. by giving her all the
furniture, and leaving her to do as she liked; while I went back to my writing,
which pays much better, though Mr. F. did say, "Stick to your teaching; you
can't write." Being willful, I said, "I won't teach; and I can write, and I'll
prove it."

June, July, August. — Wrote two tales for L. I enjoy romancing to suit myself; and
though my tales are silly, they are not bad; and my sinners always have a good
spot somewhere. I hope it is good drill for fancy and language, for I can do
it fast; and Mr. L. says my tales are so "dramatic, vivid, and full of plot," they
are just what he wants.

September, October. — Wrote much; for brain was lively, and work paid for
readily. Rewrote last story, and sent it to L., who wants more
than I can send him. So, between blue flannel
jackets for "our boys" and dainty slips ... I
reel off my "thrilling" tales, and mess up my
work in a queer but interesting way.

— From her journal
  Entries dated January through October, 1862

EDITH WHARTON:
MUMSY DOES NOT APPROVE

My first attempt (at age of eleven) was a novel, which began: "'Oh, how do you do, Mrs. Brown?' said Mrs. Tomkins. 'If only I had known you were going to call I should have tidied up the drawing-room'." Timorously I submitted this to my mother, and never shall I forget the sudden drop of my creative frenzy when she returned it with the icy comment: "Drawing-rooms are always tidy."

This was so crushing to a would-be novelist of manners that it shook me rudely out of my dream of writing fiction, and I turned to poetry instead. It was not thought necessary to feed my literary ambitions with foolscap, and for lack of paper I was driven to begging for the wrappings of the parcels delivered at the house.

— *A Backward Glance*, 1934

MOST OF US HAVE HEARD THE FAMED EXPRESSION "Keeping up with the Joneses," but it might come as a surprise that this doesn't refer to a hypothetical family, but Edith Wharton's parents. Born in 1862 and growing up as Edith Newbold Jones in the rarefied, late nineteenth-century world of wealth and privilege, her formative years consisted of riding, balls, coming-out parties, teas, and extended stays in Europe. Despite having homes in New York City and Newport, and the kind of money that gained them access to the finer things in life, culture and learning weren't particularly valued by her family. And though she lacked for nothing, it was a less-than-ideal upbringing for a bookish, dreamy girl:

"I was contented enough with swimming and riding, with my dogs, and my reading and dreaming, but I longed to travel and see new places ... and especially to being regarded as 'grown up.' I had not long to wait, for when I was seventeen my parents decided that I spent too much time in reading, and that I was to come out a year before the accepted age."

Her early attempt to gain approval for writing was almost comical, if it wasn't so sad. No wonder Wharton struggled to feel worthy of the profession. Not only was encouragement absent from her early efforts, but her family made it clear that writing was a wasteful, embarrassing pursuit for a proper society girl.

"WITHOUT PASSION, ONE WRITES IN THE AIR, OR on the sands of the seashore," wrote short story master Katherine Mansfield (1888–1923). Had Anaïs Nin encountered this quote, she would have taken it to heart, for hers was the very embodiment of a passion-fueled writing life. Born in France in 1903, Nin spent her teens living in the U.S., becoming self-educated and working as a model and dancer before returning to Europe in the 1920s. Nin had a taste for turbulence, intertwining her life on the page with a penchant for lovers (most famously with fellow author Henry Miller as well as his wife, June) and unconventional marriages.

From the earliest of her diaries, written while still in her teens, to one of her last essays, published just a year before her death in 1977 (examples of each are at right), it's clear that writing was what she believed shaped her life and gave it meaning. Decades of writing accompanied by scant publication success is ample proof that passion was the main ingredient in her steadfast devotion to the craft.

Best known for her multi-volume series of diaries, Nin kept these journals over the span of more than thirty years (not including her *Early Diary* series). It wasn't until the 1960s that they were published to acclaim as instant feminist classics, portraying one woman's lifelong voyage of self-discovery. When Nin examined the "why" of writing, it wasn't for money or glory. Rather, it filled a need as elemental as breathing. There are numerous reasons to write; they can range from philosophical, like Nin's, to practical, like Alcott's. But no matter where you fall on that spectrum, it's easy to agree that writing is a splendid way to capture and make sense of individual experience. I can't say it better than Vita Sackville-West (1892–1962): "It is necessary to write, if the days are not to slip emptily by. How else, indeed, to clap the net over the butterfly of the moment?"

Anaïs Nin: Writing, being, and breathing

Writing to me means thinking, digging, pondering, creating, shattering. It means getting at the meaning of all things; it means reaching climaxes; it means moral and spiritual and physical life all in one. Writing implies manual labor, a strain on one's conscience and an exercise of the mind ... Yes, my life flows into ink! And I am pleased. For I can live others' lives without incurring the danger of smothering my inner thought life.

— Anaïs Nin
*The Early Diaries
of Anaïs Nin,* 1921

Why one writes I can answer easily, having so often asked it of myself. I believe one writes because one has to create a world in which one can live. I could not live in any of the worlds offered to me — the world of my parents, the world of war, the world of politics. I had to create a world of my own, like a climate, a country, an atmosphere in which I could breathe, reign, and recreate myself when destroyed by living. That, I believe, is the reason for every work of art.

We also write to heighten our own awareness of life. We write to lure and enchant and console others. We write to serenade our lovers. We write to taste life twice, in the moment and in retrospection. We write, like Proust, to render all of it eternal, and to persuade ourselves that it is eternal. We write to be able to transcend our life, to reach beyond it. We write to teach ourselves to speak with others, to record the journey into the labyrinth. We write to expand our world when we feel strangled, or constricted, or lonely. We write as the birds sing, as the primitives dance their rituals. If you do not breathe through writing, if you do not cry out in writing, or sing in writing, then don't write, because our culture has no use for it. When I don't write, I feel my world shrinking. I feel I am in a prison. I feel I lose my fire and my color. It should be a necessity, as the sea needs to heave, and I call it breathing.

— *In Favor of the Sensitive Man and Other Essays,* 1976

CHAPTER TWO | *Developing a Voice*

*T*he business of writing is a
personal problem and must be
worked out in an individual way.
A great many people, ambitious
to write, fall by the wayside, but
if they are the discourageable
kind it is better that they drop
out. No beginner knows what
[she] has to go through with or
[she] would never begin.

— Willa Cather
    Interview, *Lincoln Daily Star*, 1915

In the early stages of their writing lives, the Literary Ladies in this book had no writer's conferences, writing groups, or MFA programs. In fact, only Cather, Montgomery, and L'Engle were college grads; Virginia Woolf took a few courses, and the rest did not attend at all. There were few communities of support in which a woman could develop as a writer.

Instead, what writers had in times past was a wealth of paying outlets (far more than exist today) for the written word. That's where writers, male and female, honed their skills. There were literary journals galore, popular magazines that published fiction, essays, and poetry, and newspapers that ran more than just news. The authors in this book and their contemporaries worked as journalists, reporters, critics, editors, magazine short-story writers, pamphlet-fillers, and essayists. Writing for a living was not only feasible but served as an effective apprenticeship for writers past as a way to develop and sharpen their voices.

In place of earlier forms of apprenticeship, today's writers increasingly develop their voices and skills in academic settings, workshops, conferences, and writers' groups. Will such largely unpaid (and often unread) venues be as effective for developing a generation of talented writers? Only time will tell, but any outlet that allows you to write, write, write in order to reveal your essential writing voice, makes Cather's advice at right as timely today as it was in 1915.

The dilemma for women who love to write may not have so much to do with finding the elusive literary voice, as with being reluctant to use the one that's already lurking inside, just waiting for the chance to speak up. Many of us, especially those from the generations taught to be good, accommodating girls, are afraid of sounding too strong, too loud, too unconventional, or simply too much like the self we're afraid to reveal to the world. Most of us have at least an inkling of what form our writing voice should take, if only we might find the courage to reveal it.

WILLA CATHER:
A WRITING VOICE REVEALED

When I was in college and immediately after graduation, I did newspaper work. I found that newspaper writing did a great deal of good for me in working off the purple flurry of my early writing. Every young writer has to work off the "fine writing" stage. It was a painful period in which I overcame my florid, exaggerated, foamy-at-the-mouth, adjective-spree period. I knew even then it was a crime to write like I did, but I had to get the adjectives and the youthful fervor worked off.

I believe every young writer must write whole books of extravagant language to get it out. It is agony to be smothered in your own florescence, and to be forced to dump great cartloads of your posies out in the road before you find that one posy that will fit in the right place...

— Interview, *Lincoln Daily Star,* 1915

WILLA CATHER:
IS IMITATION A GOOD WAY TO LEARN?

 When I was in college, I admired
certain writers and read the masters of style,
who gave me great pleasure. Those ideas have
changed. All students imitate, and I began by imitating
Henry James. He was the most interesting American
who was writing at the time, and I strove laboriously
to pattern after him ... it is a perfectly right form of
education. It takes a long time to get out from under
the traditions which hamper a young writer. It is a
recognized fact that young painters should imitate the
work of the great masters, but people overlook the
fact that it is equally dangerous, however, to try to be
"original" too early.

— Interview, *New York World*, 1925

DISTINGUISH WHAT IS YOUR OWN

 In "Alexander's Bridge" I was still
more preoccupied with trying to write
well than with anything else. A painter or
writer must learn to distinguish what is [her] own
from what [she] admires. I never abandoned trying
to compromise between the kinds of matter which my
experience had given me, and the kind of writing I
admired, until I began my second novel, *O Pioneers!*.

— Interview, *The New Yorker*, 1931

IN ANNE LAMOTT'S WITTY CONTEMPORARY classic on becoming a writer, *Bird by Bird* (1995), she bemoans the effects of literary influences on her writing students: "Every time Isabel Allende has a new book out, I'm happy because I will get to read it, and I'm unhappy because half of my students are going to start writing like her ... But their renditions never ring true, any more than they ring true a few months later when Ann Beattie's latest book arrives and my students start submitting stories about shiny bowls and windowpanes."

Finding one's unique voice is quite possibly the most essential task in the journey to becoming a writer. Some of our Literary Ladies advised giving into the influences of other writers and gleaning valuable lessons from them until your own style and voice emerge. Like art students copying Old Masters, you learn fundamentals from the best teachers on the path before you. At left, Willa Cather unabashedly admits to imitating Henry James. She may have been overzealous; her first novel, *Alexander's Bridge*, was criticized as derivative. Edith Wharton, likewise, was immensely influenced by James, her friend and correspondent. At right, she, too, encourages a phase of imitation and influence. But when critics hinted at James's influence on her writing, she bristled defensively.

Imitation and influence are inevitable and have their advantages as well as perils. Eudora Welty (1909–2001) provides another perspective: "Since we must and do write each in our own way, we may during actual writing get more lasting instruction not from another's work, whatever its blessings, however better it is than ours, but from our own poor scratched-over pages. For these we can hold up to life. That is, we are born with a mind and heart to hold each page up to and to ask: Is it valid?"

Every dawning talent has to go through a phase of imitation and subjection to influences, and the great object of the young writer should be not to fear those influences, but to seek only the greatest, and to assimilate them so they become [her] stock-in-trade.

— Edith Wharton
   From a letter, 1918

WILLA CATHER: IMAGINATION REFLECTS EXPERIENCE

 The young writer must learn to deal with subjects [she] really knows about. No matter how commonplace a subject may be, if it is one with which the author is thoroughly familiar it makes a much better story than the purely imaginational.

Imagination, which is a quality writers must have, does not mean the ability to weave pretty stories out of nothing. In the right sense, imagination is a response to what is going on — a sensitiveness to which outside things appeal. It is a composition of sympathy and observation.

— Interview, *Lincoln Daily Star*, 1915

CHARLOTTE BRONTË: IMAGINATION AUGMENTS REALITY

 Is not the real experience of each individual very limited? And, if a writer dwells upon that solely or principally, is [she] not in danger of repeating [herself], and also becoming an egotist? Then, too, imagination is a strong, restless faculty, which claims to be heard and exercised: are we to be quite deaf to her cry, and insensate to her struggles? When she shows us bright pictures, are we never to look at them, and try to reproduce them? And when she is eloquent, and speaks rapidly and urgently in our ear, are we not to write to her dictation?

— From a letter to G.H. Lewes, 1848

A rare photo of Charlotte Brontë

WHEN DEVELOPING A LITERARY VOICE, SHOULD WRITERS HEED THE most hackneyed directive of writing instruction, to "write what you know," or is it better to plunge into the world of imagination? Charlotte Brontë and Willa Cather have two different takes on this.

Willa Cather was born in Winchester, Virginia in 1873. When she was nine years old, her family moved to Red Cloud, Nebraska; it was this immersion into the pioneering world of poor European immigrants that inspired some of her best-known works. Recognizing her talent for writing, some of her college classmates secretly submitted an essay she wrote to the *Nebraska State Journal*. Seeing her work in print promptly changed her plans: "Up to that time I had planned to specialize in medicine ... But what youthful vanity can be unaffected by the sight of itself in print! It was a kind of hypnotic effect."

Like many other authors, Willa Cather first worked as a journalist, starting with a position at the *Nebraska State Journal* while still a college student in the 1890s. Her first postgraduate job was on the editorial staff of *McClure's* magazine in New York City, where she worked her way up to managing editor. She credits the fast pace of newspaper and magazine production for helping her to work off what she aptly describes in the previous chapter as the "purple flurry" of early writing attempts. When New England author Sarah Orne Jewett (1849–1909) became Willa Cather's mentor, she urged her to shed her fixation on writing like Henry James, and to mine the memories of her youth in Red Cloud for material. The prairies and immigrant families of her childhood home inspired the classics *My Ántonia* and *O Pioneers!*.

Charlotte Brontë questions whether individual experiences are too limiting, and in her own case, this was true. Without succumbing to the "strong, restless faculty" that was her imagination, how would the daughter of a village cleric have written the sweeping gothic, *Jane Eyre*? Though Brontë leaned toward imagination, she incorporated her actual experiences as a teacher and governess to flesh out her heroine's journey. And while Cather favored the idea of writing about that which was familiar, she injected her realism with fully imagined events and characters.

Current interpretations of "write what you know" are more helpful and less trite: Write what you want to know (if it interests you, it may interest your readers); write about what you love, or what you care about most deeply. Marrying the worlds of reality and imagination, when done thoughtfully, can result in narratives that sound authentic, whether set on the streets of your home town, or an imagined planet in a distant galaxy.

IN THE CANON OF THE GREATEST AUTHORS OF English literature, Virginia Woolf occupies a permanent spot. Considered far ahead of her time as an innovator within the novelistic framework, she recognized the experimental nature of her works even as she wrote them. Her life and work continue to be subjects of endless interpretation, art, analysis, and academic study.

Born Adeline Virginia Stephen in London in 1882, her father (shown with her in the photo at right) was a literary critic, and her mother a renowned beauty and artists' model. Her mother's sudden death when Virginia was thirteen may have been the catalyst for the first of her recurrent nervous breakdowns. Enveloped in the fertile intellectual atmosphere of the Bloomsbury circle (a group of progressive thinkers that included her sister, artist Vanessa Bell), Woolf might well have achieved an enviable writer's life if not for debilitating battles with mental illness. But this wasn't the only source of anguish. She was eternally self-critical, restless, and rarely satisfied with her efforts.

As a young woman, Woolf developed her writer's voice with a number of literary pursuits. She reviewed books for the *Times Literary Supplement,* wrote scores of articles and essays, and for a short time, taught English and history at Morley College in London (though she herself hadn't earned a degree).

While still in her twenties, she embarked on writing her first novel, whose working title was *Melymbrosia.* Begun in 1907, it was eventually completed and published in 1915, after seven and a half years of toil, as *The Voyage Out.* Despite daunting challenges, she left behind not only ten novels (all considered classics), but copious numbers of nonfiction books and essays. Her autobiographical and diaristic writings shed light on a consummate artist's process. Her iconic line from *A Room of One's Own,* "A woman must have money and a room of her own if she is to write fiction," still resonates today.

O why do I ever let anyone read what I write! Every time I have to go through a breakfast with a letter of criticism I swear I will write for my own praise or blame in future. It is a misery.

— Virginia Woolf
From a letter to a friend
(Violet Dickinson), 1907

Virginia Woolf: "My writing makes me tremble"

 My writing makes me tremble ... I have wasted all my time trying to begin things and taking up different points of view, and dropping them, and grinding out the dullest stuff, which makes my blood run thick. However, I shall begin again now, I have 4 books of white paper waiting me.

— From a letter to a friend (Violet Dickinson), 1907

"My boldness terrifies me"

 I will offer some explanation of the wretched first volume ... When I read the thing over (one very grey evening) I thought it so flat and monotonous that I did not even feel "the atmosphere": certainly there was no character in it. Next morning I proceeded to slash and rewrite, in the hope of animating it; and (as I suspect for I have not re-read it) destroyed the one virtue it had — a kind of continuity; for I wrote it originally in a dream-like state, which was at any rate, unbroken. My intention now is to write straight on, and finish the book, and then, if that day ever comes, to catch if possible the first imagination and go over the beginning again with broad touches, keeping much of the original draft, and trying to deepen the atmosphere — giving the feel of running water, and not much else.

… I admit the justice of your hint that sometimes I have had an inkling of the way the book might be written by other people. It is very difficult to fight against it; as difficult as to ignore the opinion of one's probable readers — I think I gather courage as I go on. The only possible reason for writing down all this, is that it represents roughly a view of one's own. My boldness terrifies me. I feel I have so few of the gifts that make novels amusing.

— From a letter to her brother-in-law (Clive Bell), 1909

Edna Ferber: "The life of my imagination"

"*That novel about Texas — is that the story of your life?*"
"That novel about New England — is that the story of your life?"
"That novel about Alaska — is that the story of your life?"

...When readers of these books write or speak to me, asking if this is the story of my life, I am far from irked or resentful. I am flattered. It means that these fictional lives, these characters that never existed except in my imagination, actually have taken on such proportions of reality that the reader believes them to have been formed on fact; and that the tragic and comic and everyday events described in the novels took place in real life. Not only that — in the story-teller's real life. What can a writer wish for more splendid than to know that by putting those little black marks on a sheet of blank white paper there have been accepted in the mind of the reader human beings with three dimensions who walk talk breathe live suffer exult die, much as the reader has done or will do, or has observed in his fellow men.

Is this, they ask, the story of your life?

Yes. My inner life. The life of my imagination and creative ability.

Writing is lonely work but the creative writer is rarely alone. The room in which one works is peopled with the men and women and children of the writer's imagination. Often they are difficult — but rarely boring — company. This is a fortunate thing, for they are with one day and night, they never leave while the book or play is in progress. One wishes sometimes that they would go away. Just leave me alone for an hour — a minute — won't you! Often they are so much more fascinating to the writer than the living people one actually encounters that to go to a party, a dinner, even to the theatre is an anti-climax. Every day for hours one is shut up in a room with a company of chosen people created by oneself. It is a pattern of self-immolation familiar to any writer worth reading. The writer does not even remotely look upon this as a hardship. It is a way of life; a necessary and chosen way of life. Witty conversation, purposely dull dialogue, love, murder, marriage, birth, violence, triumph, failure, death — anything can happen in that room.

— Edna Ferber, *A Kind of Magic,* 1963

EDNA FERBER IS LESS KNOWN AS AN AUTHOR today than are many of the others in this book. Yet in her time and place (her prodigious output spanned mainly from the 1920s to the 1950s), she was an independent, powerful woman whose books' success gave her a great deal of clout in film and theater. Her works were financial gold mines. Though her fiction and theatrical work may now be deemed more "popular" than literary, within her accessible storylines she spoke out against discrimination and classism, and created bold female protagonists.

Ferber was born in Kalamazoo, Michigan in 1885, the daughter of working-class immigrants. Her family moved around the midwest before settling in Appleton, Wisconsin, where she spent her teen years. Her senior essays so impressed the editor of the *Appleton Daily Crescent* that he offered the seventeen-year-old Ferber a reporting job. And so, a career was born. In due time, she moved up to a reporter's position at the *Milwaukee Journal*. She gradually intertwined her newspaper work with short story writing. Her first novel, *Dawn O'Hara,* was the tale of a newspaper reporter in Milwaukee — following the grand tradition of writing what you know. Soon enough, she began spinning stories of realms much further afield.

Ferber's reputation was cemented with *So Big* (1924), which was not only a bestseller, but which won that year's Pulitzer Prize for the Novel (as it was then called). So panoramic were her narratives that fully eight of her thirteen novels became major movies, including *Giant, Show Boat,* and the classic western, *Cimmaron.* She also wrote eight plays, some of which were produced on Broadway, and numerous short stories. Becoming a writer, for Ferber, meant living comfortably in the realm of imagination and surrounding herself with colleagues from publishing, film, and the theater.

PUBLISHED AUTHORS ARE OFTEN ASKED "HOW DO you get your ideas?" It's a question that defies an easy answer, if it can be answered at all. Most often, ideas seem to find you, not the other way around. Of course, something you see, hear, or read can ignite sparks of inspiration, but the day-to-day work habits you develop can fuel the cultivating of imagination.

On the page facing, Louisa May Alcott and Willa Cather share similar techniques for nourishing ideas. They allowed seedlings of ideas to blossom within before setting them to paper, recognizing, perhaps, that imagination has its own power to operate side by side with the conscious process. For many women authors, working in this manner was a way to juggle duty with a writing schedule; the practical necessity of thinking out plots and characters became a favored technique. L.M. Montgomery, in fact, called this method "brooding up" a story, and used it to great advantage for much of her writing life, both as a working girl, and later as a working mother. Other authors have spoken of allowing ideas to brew while doing mundane activities, rather than forcing them out while sitting at the writing desk. Agatha Christie, for example, thought that the best time to plan a book was while doing the dishes.

For anyone who doesn't have the luxury of long hours to spend at the writing desk, it's comforting to know that your head can serve as your study, as Louisa May Alcott describes it, and that you can carry this portable work space wherever you go. Allowing fledgling ideas to mature before committing them to paper may help them emerge more fully formed.

LOUISA MAY ALCOTT: "MY HEAD IS MY STUDY"

 My methods of work are very simple and soon told. My head is my study, & there I keep the various plans of stories for years some times, letting them grow as they will till I am ready to put them on paper. Then it is quick work, as chapters go down word for word as they stand in my mind & need no alteration. I never copy, since I find by experience that the work I spend the least time upon is best liked by critics & readers...

While a story is under way I lie in it, see the people, more plainly than the real ones, round me, hear them talk, & am much interested, surprised, or provoked at their actions, for I seem to have no power to rule them, & can simply record their experiences & performances.

— From a letter to journalist Frank Carpenter, 1887

WILLA CATHER: THE STORY IS IN THE INK BOTTLE

 What I write results from a personal explosional experience. All of a sudden, the idea for a story is in my head. It is in the ink bottle when I start to write. But I don't start until the idea has found its own pattern and fixed its proper tone. And it does that; some of the things that I first consider important fade into insignificance, while others that I first glimpse as minor things, grow until they show that they are the important things. It seems a natural process...a novel should be like a symphony, developed from one theme, one dominating tone.

— Interview, *San Francisco Chronicle,* 1931

MADELEINE L'ENGLE:
LETTING IDEAS SIMMER SLOWLY

 When I start working on a book, which is usually several years and several books before I start to write it, I am somewhat like a French peasant cook. There are several pots on the back of the stove, and as I go by during the day's work, I drop a carrot in one, an onion in another, a chunk of meat in another. When it comes time to prepare the meal, I take the pot which is nearly full and bring it to the front of the stove.

So it is with writing. There are several pots on those back burners. An idea for a scene goes into one, a character into another, a description of a tree in the fog into another. When it comes time to write, I bring forward the pot which has the most in it. The dropping of ideas is sometimes quite conscious; sometimes it happens without my realizing it. I look and something has been added which is just what I need, but I don't remember when it was added.

When it is time to start work, I look at everything in the pot, sort, arrange, think about character and story line. Most of this part of the work is done consciously, but then there comes a moment of unselfconsciousness, of letting go and serving the work.

— *Walking on Water,* 1980

THE MOST CONTEMPORARY AUTHOR AMONG THE dozen Literary Ladies is Madeleine L'Engle. Like the others, she's no longer with us, though she's the only one who lived into the twenty-first century. A native of New York City, L'Engle was born in 1918, the only child of creative parents who encouraged her talents. Though her writing ability emerged quite early, she was labeled shy, clumsy, and even dull-witted in school, and those experiences, not surprisingly, had lasting effects on her self-esteem.

Best known for the young adult fantasy classic *A Wrinkle in Time* (and its successors, *A Wind in the Door, A Swiftly Tilting Planet,* along with many other books and series), L'Engle shared both philosophical musings and practical writing advice in her memoirs. In them she recounted years of bruising rejection, as well as the challenges of raising children while literary ambition burned bright.

How I love and relate to L'Engle's culinary metaphor at left describing how she "cooks up" plots for her books (though in my case, the chunk of meat would be a hunk of tofu!). Whether L'Engle's "burners" were in her head in or a series of notebooks we never find out, but this passage reinforces the notion that some ideas need a long, slow back burner treatment, sometimes to simmer for years at a time — ever in the background, but not forgotten. It's not unusual for a writer or any sort of creative person to cycle back to an idea that was a mere seedling years or even decades in the past.

Creative projects that stubbornly refuse to pull together — sometimes for seemingly indefinable reasons — might well need more time to percolate in the backround of a busy mind. Rushing ideas onto the page or into print might yield results that are (to use another culinary metaphor) half-baked.

A NUMBER OF BOOKS FOR ASPIRING WRITERS PRESENT SCENARIOS IN which budding wordsmiths do battle with naysayers: parents who threaten to disown, partners who consider them nut cases, and teachers who pronounce them talentless. Case in point: "Your girlfriend, boyfriend, or spouse will put up with this writer-talk for weeks, months, or even years, but none of them will love you for it," writes Carolyn See in *Making a Literary Life.* "Your writing, to them, is like a case of genital herpes. It's possible for them to love you, but they'll have to overlook the writing." While I'm sure that this happens occasionally, I doubt it's generally as dire as that; maybe this kind of drama makes for better copy.

All of the Literary Ladies had at least one person, if not several, who supported and stood by them. For some it was a like-minded colleague or group of colleagues; for others it was a spouse or lover, or an entire family. Some of these alliances were lifelong, and in other instances they shifted to suit various phases in a particular author's life. What's key is that women who ultimately succeeded as writers chose to align themselves with supporters, not detractors. Not everyone will have a family whose enthusiasm matches the Alcott's. But if the circle into which you're born is less than thrilled with your avocation, you can choose a different support system, like Edith Wharton did.

Young Louisa May Alcott wrote many poems, sketches, and plays for the amusement of her family and their group of intellectual friends. They applauded and exclaimed over her every effort, much as their fictional counterparts did in *Little Women.* No one was more supportive than her beloved "Marmee." Alcott dedicated her first book of short stories (*Flower Fables)* to her with the rather grandiose inscription "the first fruits of my genius." The first serious novel she released under her own name (*Moods,* 1864) seemed an extension of her need to please and entertain those she loved, even as she worked on it. Between the writing of *Moods* and its publication were a stint as a Civil War nurse, a bout with typhoid pneumonia (whose treatment with a mercury-based medicine permanently damaged her health), and a protracted editorial process on the manuscript (which the author felt damaged its integrity —and her own; once she was famous, she re-released the novel in a form closer to its original). Later rejecting any notions of "genius," she let her desire to financially support her family, who had supported her creatively, continue to galvanize her writing career.

LOUISA MAY ALCOTT: AIMING TO PLEASE

 February, 1861 — *Another* turn at "Moods," which I remodeled. From the 2nd to the 25th I sat writing, with a run at dusk; could not sleep, and for three days was so full of it I could not stop to get up...Read all I had done to my family; and Father said "Emerson must see this. Where did you get your metaphysics?" Mother pronounced it wonderful, and Anna laughed and cried, as she always does, over my works, saying, "My dear, I'm proud of you."

So I had a good time, even if it never comes to anything; for it was worth something to have my three dearest sit up till midnight listening with wide-open eyes to Lu's first novel. I planned it some time ago, and have had it in my mind ever so long; but now it begins to take shape.

— From her journal
   Entry dated February 1861

Alcott House, Concord, Massachusetts

AMONG ALL THE LITERARY LADIES, ONLY EDITH Wharton had out-and-out disapproval from those closest to her, including her mother and society friends, who thought that literary pursuits were beneath a person of her class. Nothing but indifference came from her early, failed marriage to society gadfly Teddy Wharton. She was, of all the Ladies, the most vocal about her lack of confidence. Her insecurity over her talent and abilities was overcome at last by the building of small successes, as well as the welcome friendship and constructive critique of one who did believe in her talent. Walter Berry became a confidant for whom she carried a torch for life (and perhaps beyond, as his Paris grave is next to hers). Later, she formed a literary alliance with Henry James, who was a treasured friend and correspondent, as well.

Charlotte Brontë and her sisters formed a circle of mutual support; Jane Austen's father and brothers were completely invested in seeing her work published (and in fact acted as her representatives). I can think of no spouse more supportive than Leonard Woolf, and Madeleine L'Engle's husband softened the blows when rejection piled upon rejection. Calvin Stowe, though never much help, greatly esteemed his wife's talent and wrote to her, "My dear, you must be a literary woman ... write yourself only and always, Harriet Beecher Stowe, which is a name euphonious, flowing, and full of meaning." Willa Cather found a worthy mentor in author Sarah Orne Jewett, who gave her much encouragement and advice. In terms of literary achievement, the student soon surpassed the teacher.

The Literary Ladies amply demonstrate the benefits of being surrounded by believers who aren't mere cheerleaders, but who offer perspective and constructive mentoring, especially when a writing voice is emerging.

Edith Wharton:
The value of a believing mentor

 Though I was always interested in what was said of my books, and sometimes (though rarely) helped by the comments of the professional critics, never did they influence me against my judgment, or deflect me by a hair's-breadth from what I knew to be "the real right" way.

In this I was much helped by Walter Berry. No critic was ever severer, but none had more respect for the artist's liberty. He taught me never to be satisfied with my own work, but never to let my inward conviction as to the rightness of anything I had done be affected by outside opinion...

He alone not only encouraged me to write, as others had already done, but had the patience and intelligence to teach me how ... His invariable rule, though he prized above all things concision and austerity, was to encourage me to write as my own instinct impelled me; and it was only after the story or the book was done that we set out together on the "adjective hunts" from which we often brought back such heavy bags.

Once I had found my footing and had my material in hand, his criticisms became increasingly searching. With each book he exacted a higher standard in economy of expression, in purity of language, in the avoidance of the hackneyed and the precious.

— *A Backward Glance*, 1934

Was She Justified In Seeking A Divorce?

Why was this American girl forced to leave her brutal Polish husband? Why did Ellen, Countess Olenska, return to New York, seeking to forget? Whispers came all too soon that she had been compromised in the artistic continental society from which she had fled. But in the narrow New York society of the 1870's she was welcomed back, and the whispers of far off Europe ignored, until she and Newland Archer are swept together by mutual attraction, and the old, old question is renewed, shall she create a scandal just because she is unhappy?

All the glamor of the society life of the original Four Hundred is the background for this story, the nights at the opera, the balls, the intimate amusements of the society leaders of the day. Newland Archer's life is spent among them, and Ellen, with her charm of other lands, comes to him as a breath of a new day. But he is firm-rooted in cramped New York, a girl of his own circle, and his whole standing of the moral values of the situation is presented with a sure understanding of the moral values of the situation is presented with a sure understanding of the moral values of the situation is presented with a sure understanding. things that lure them, these children of New York's Age of Innocence.

THE AGE OF INNOCENCE

By Edith Wharton

This is a full length novel by the foremost American woman novelist, which in strength and breadth of appeal rivals "The House of Mirth." It is entertaining from the opening scene at the Opera in New York to the last pages laid in Paris. The leading characters appear as living human beings against the keen pictures of society, and the book, as a whole, will take its place beside "The House of Mirth" as the outstanding depiction of New York Society.

"The Age of Innocence" represents Mrs. Wharton's art at its pinnacle. All her splendid abilities find their choicest material in this her greatest novel, and in it she has given the world of readers a book that is unsurpassed for entertaining qualities. $2.00 *net.*

[3]

America's Greatest Woman Novelist

"The foremost American novelist." — *Boston Transcript.*

"Paul Bourget calls her the greatest American novelist." — *New York Sun.*

"A book from her leading novelist's pen is an event." — *Philadelphia Public Led ger.*

"Mrs. Wharton's touch is the deftest, the surest, of all our American novelists to-day." — *The New Republic.*

"Edith of Mrs. Wharton's later novels has represented a new and different handling..." — *Quarterly Review.*

CHAPTER THREE | *Tools of the Trade*

To be a professional writer one must be prepared to give up almost everything except living …The first lesson to be learned by a writer is to be able to say, "Thanks so much. I'd love to, but I can't. I'm working."

— Edna Ferber,
A Kind of Magic, 1963

THIS CHAPTER EXPLORES THE NUTS AND BOLTS OF WRITING. LIKE any craft, writing requires a few essential tools, but unlike a potter's studio or a woodshop, the tools of this trade (other than your computer, or, if you're a Luddite, a typewriter) are invisible. The tools that kept the Literary Ladies in top form were discipline, good work habits (which include regular practice to keep one's writing mind limber and prevent writer's block), and a fairly regular writing schedule. Some degree of privacy has always been desirable, if it could be managed, but a lack thereof was not always a hindrance.

A famous writerly quote goes something like: "The art of writing is the art of applying the seat of the pants to the seat of the chair." Attributed to Mary Heaton Vorse (1874–1966), variations of it have been credited to (mostly male) authors from Ernest Hemingway to Kingsley Amis.

If only it was that simple. The obscure Ms. Vorse plied her trade in an era when the only thing between a writer and the typewriter or notebook on her desk was the blank page. Now, that page is on the computer screen, and behind it, the entire universe on the Web, seducing you with endless distractions. It's hard to quantify whether it's more difficult to be disciplined now, when there are an infinite number of ways to procrastinate, than it was one or two hundred years ago. If inclined to dawdle, a literary woman in the nineteenth century could just as easily have found a myriad of reasons to avoid writing. There were chickens to be plucked, babies to be swaddled, and infirm elderly parents to attend to.

Edna Ferber saw no obstacles to her own practice that couldn't be overcome by discipline and steady work. Her advice on getting work done is timeless: don't get overwhelmed by the big picture; chip away at your task one manageable chunk at a time. This self-mastery stands in contrast to the iconic image of the dissolute, testosterone-driven male writer of genius, embodied by the likes of Kerouac and Faulkner. Through her novels' strong female characters, Ferber encouraged women to live larger, bolder lives. If she were still with us, she'd accept no excuses — and no nonsense — from today's writing women.

Edna Ferber: Discipline, a day at a time

 The born writer goes to [her] desk daily and remains there throughout certain fixed hours each day. Sometimes ten words manage to get themselves down on paper, sometimes a page or two, sometimes (rarely) five or even more...

If, after months and sometimes years of research, of notes, of a first rough copy, you begin to try to assemble this amorphous body into some semblance of form, begin the actual long process of writing in order and in sequence, it is better (for me, at least) to think of it only in terms of one day; today's work only. Each day three pages, two pages, even but one on a bad day; and sometimes all of it to be rewritten next day and often rewritten and rewritten.

It is better to think of a novel or any long piece of work as a day to day task to be done, no matter how eagerly you may think ahead (when you're not actually putting words to paper) to the chapters not yet written. It is a long journey, to be undertaken sometimes with hope and confidence and high spirits; sometimes with despair. If one thinks of it in terms of four hundred — four hundred and fifty — five hundred pages, one can drown in a morass of apprehension. So one step after another, slowly, painfully, but a step. And so it grows. You have felt or observed in life something that you want terribly to say, and you want to say it more than you want to do anything else in the world.

— *A Kind of Magic*, 1963

MADELEINE L'ENGLE: "I MUST SEIZE OPPORTUNITIES"

 Many people in walks of life which do not involve creation are completely unaware of the necessity for discipline. It is not only that few serious artists who live lives of debauchery produce a large body of work but that few serious artists are able to live lives which are without interruption.

To write consistently, I must seize opportunities. I write in airports. I write on planes. I find airports and planes and hotels excellent places in which to write because once I am in them I am not responsible for anything except my work. Once I have my seat assignment I can write until the flight is called; when I am on the plane, the pilot is responsible for the flight, I am not, and so I can work on my manuscript. In a hotel room I do not have to think about the vacuum cleaner...domestic chores are not my responsibility; I am free to write.

— *Walking on Water*, 1980

"ULTIMATELY, YOU HAVE TO SIT DOWN AND START..."

 Ultimately, you have to sit down and start to write. And even if all you do is type out "I can't write this morning; I can't write this morning; oh, bother, I can't write this morning," that will sometimes prime the pump and get it started. It is a matter of discipline. It is particularly a matter of discipline for a woman who has children or another job.

I think my years in the English boarding school where I had to create my own privacy were also a way of learning to create my own discipline. Now there are mornings when I joyfully sit down at the typewriter. But there are mornings when it is anything but a joy. There are evenings when I go to the piano and the music comes pouring from my fingers. There are evenings when I'm all thumbs and I have to make myself sit there and go over scales and finger exercises before I can play anything. The same thing is true with writing.

— *Madeleine L'Engle Herself*, 2001

MADELEINE L'ENGLE'S FIRST CAREER CHOICE upon graduating from Smith College in 1941 was to be an actress. She soon found modest success in Broadway roles. By 1945 she had written a handful of plays that were produced, as well as a published but largely forgotten first novel, *The Small Rain*. After these modest steps toward success, L'Engle's career hit a wall in the 1950s when she struggled to reconcile her ambitions with the return of more traditional gender roles in post-World War II America. She wanted a full family life as well as a writing career a couple of decades before the phrase "having it all" came into use. From her memoirs, it's easy to glean that discipline and perseverance were constant companions.

From the quote at right, you might correctly assume that L'Engle was deeply religious. But you need not be religious to appreciate how viewing discipline from a spiritual perspective might temper its severe reputation, which conjures up an image of a strict schoolmarm who's going to rap your knuckles with a ruler if you don't buckle down. L'Engle's view instead makes the concept more soothing, transforming it into an artist's best hedge against the uncertainty and interruptions that are part of daily life. Her words serve as a reminder that discipline triggers inspiration, not the other way around.

To work on a book is for me very much the same thing as to pray. Both involve discipline … Inspiration far more often comes during the work than before it, because the largest part of the job of the artist is to listen to the work and to go where it tells [her] to go. Ultimately, when you are writing, you stop thinking and write what you hear.

— Madeleine L'Engle
Walking on Water, 1980

DESPITE PROTESTATIONS TO THE CONTRARY, GEORGE SAND FOUND the discipline to produce an immense body of work, while giving meaning to the phrase "living large." Too bad she didn't leave explicit instructions on how exactly she accomplished what she did. Though not without a healthy ego, she was quite adept at self-flagellation. I hope that wasn't the secret of her success, but if that turns out to be the case, then I have a good head start, as I regularly beat myself up (metaphorically, of course) for not doing enough.

You can be sure that the Masterpiece Theatre version of Sand's life focused more on her adventures in the bedroom than at her desk, as in the former venue she was also prolific. Her most notable liaison was with legendary composer Frédéric Chopin, and her most controversial affair was with the glamorous actress Marie Dorval. Sand preferred younger men and enjoyed plenty of them; Her *nom de plume* was inspired by one such lover, Jules Sandeau, with whom she collaborated on a few stories.

Sand had her legions of devotees, but her few detractors were vocal. One of them was the poet Charles Baudelaire (1821–1867), who wrote of her, "The fact that there are men who could become enamoured of this slut is indeed a proof of the abasement of the men of this generation." Colette (1873–1954), however, reflected on her countrywoman with envy and awe: "How the devil did George Sand manage? That sturdy woman of letters found it possible to finish one novel and start another in the same hour. And she did not thereby lose either a lover or a puff of the *narghile* [hookah], not to mention a *Story of My Life* in twenty volumes ..." No literary slacker herself, Colette was equally adept at self-flagellation: "Writing is often wasteful. If I counted the pages I've torn up, of how many volumes am I the author?"

George Sand seemed as peeved at herself for giving in to distractions as I imagine today's dilly-dallying scribes might be when the temptations of Facebook win out over getting some work done. Yet despite Sand's torrents of prose, there are now more books in print about her life than there are in-print translations of her work. Her colorful character and individuality seem to have eclipsed her literary legacy. Not to diminish her accomplishments, but in the end, perhaps in spite of herself she proved that for some, at least, it's more important to be courageous and original in one's life than to be prolific in one's work.

George Sand:
Fighting distraction, nineteenth-century style

 While you are running around to get material for your novel, I am inventing all sorts of pretexts not to write mine. I let myself be distracted by guilty fancies, something I am reading fascinates me and I set myself to scribbling on paper that will be left in my desk and bring me no return. That has amused me, or rather that has compelled me, for it would be in vain for me to struggle against these caprices; they interrupt me and force me...you see that I have not the strength of mind that you think.

— From a letter to Gustave Flaubert, 1869

For the present I am overwhelmed with work; work which, unfortunately, is very barren in its results. I still live in hope. Besides, see how strange it is: literature becomes a passion. The more obstacles, the more difficulties you perceive, the more ambitious you are of overcoming them.

— George Sand, *from a letter to a friend, 1831*

Anaïs Nin: Practice becomes talent

 I didn't have any particular gift in my twenties. I didn't have any exceptional qualities. It was the persistence and the great love of my craft which finally became a discipline, which finally made me a craftsman and a writer.

The only reason I finally was able to say exactly what I felt was because, like a pianist practicing, I wrote every day. There was no more than that. There was no studying of writing, there was no literary discipline, there was only the reading and receiving of experience...

So I would like to remove from everyone the feeling that writing is something that is only done by a few gifted people ... You shouldn't think that someone who achieves fulfillment in writing and a certain art in writing is necessarily a person with unusual gifts. I always said it was an unusual stubbornness. Nothing prevented me from doing it every night, after every day's happenings.

— From "The Personal Life Deeply Lived,"
  Lecture, 1975

SO, HOW EXACTLY DOES A WRITER DEVELOP THE discipline to sit down on a regular basis and get some decent writing done? It's a question that has no simple answer, but writing guides from Dorothea Brande's seminal *Becoming a Writer* (1934) through the myriad that continue to be published each year have suggested adhering to a consistent schedule, setting about to work at about the same time each day. This is a classic piece of advice for blasting through the resistance of "Not right now," a favorite excuse of the subconscious mind. And in turn, this regular schedule of writing becomes a practice, something Anaïs Nin recognized long before "writing practice" was popularized in writer's guides of the 1980s and 1990s, notably, Natalie Goldberg's *Writing Down the Bones* and *Wild Mind*.

Katherine Anne Porter (1890–1980), the author best known for *Ship of Fools,* also advocated writing practice as a way to keep the mind nimble: "I love to write for the sake of writing and saying what is in my mind at the time ... we are happier and do better work if we let our minds range freely through all our interests, not trying to sustain one tone, or level or mood; and everything we do helps everything else; by writing we keep limbered up, like an athlete ..."

Some of us, yours truly included, have subconscious minds that, like cats, resist any sort of training. But this method of finding a set time to write — either whatever comes to mind or some specific work — has benefitted legions of writers. It's worth a shot if you struggle with "Not right now." If you're like me and you're more of a "Not enough time" kind of gal, what you'll find on the next two pages will put that excuse to bed once and for all.

"IT IS NO LESS DIFFICULT TO WRITE SENTENCES IN A RECIPE THAN sentences in *Moby Dick*. So you might as well write *Moby Dick*," Annie Dillard claims in *The Writing Life* (1989). Oh, now she tells me, after I've written ten cookbooks! And I thought I was avoiding writing my rendition of *Moby Dick* because I didn't have the great swaths of time I believed necessary for the task. I had children to raise, and writing work that paid, so why revisit the painful task of attempting to write a novel, only to fail yet again? A number of prolific authors, some in these pages, have demonstrated that an immense body of work can be produced in a mere handful of hours per day.

In a 1921 interview in her New York City home, far from the Nebraska prairies that inspired her early classics, Willa Cather's work schedule was described as follows: "Miss Cather works but three hours a day — hours of perfect joy and happiness, she describes them ... She believes that a writer should keep in as good physical condition as a singer, and so she regulates her life on a simple, normal schedule. She writes easily and seldom tears a paragraph or a page to pieces."

Would that we could all enjoy such an angst-free schedule! However, most of us are lucky if, after two or three hours, we've written more than a few paragraphs that upon subsequent inspection don't read like sheer drivel. Let's not forget that prior to this interview Cather had already published four of her major novels, and those, after her long apprenticeship as a journalist. When she sat down at her desk for those two to three hours, she was already a seasoned writer. Despite this leisurely schedule, Cather wrote ten more novels, plus many essays and short stories.

Louisa May Alcott, on the other hand, was less than happy with the curtailed work schedule of her later career. Though she complained of being "chained to my galley," that's exactly what she preferred. L.M. Montgomery spent few hours at her desk, but worked all the time in her mind, as she described in a letter: "I write fast, having 'thought out' plot and dialogue while I go about my household work. I only do three hours' literary work a day — two hours' writing and one typewriting."

Maybe there are times in your life when, as Alcott described it, "the steam is up" and you have the time and energy to write from morning until night. There will be other times when writing two to three hours might be sufficient to get good work done. But whether your writing schedule is constrained voluntarily or by circumstances, much can be accomplished, so long as whatever time you have is spent diligently and, if at all possible, joyfully.

WILLA CATHER:
BRILLIANCE IN THREE HOURS OR LESS

 I work from two and a half to three hours a day. I don't hold myself to longer hours; if I did, I wouldn't gain by it. The only reason I write is because it interests me more than any other activity I've ever found. I like riding, going to operas and concerts, travel in the west; but on the whole writing interests me more than anything else. If I made a chore of it, my enthusiasm would die. I make it an adventure every day. I get more entertainment from it than any I could buy, except the privilege of hearing a few great musicians and singers … For me, the morning is the best time to write. During the other hours of the day I attend to my housekeeping, take walks in Central Park, go to concerts, and see something of my friends. I try to keep myself fit, fresh: one has to be in as good form to write as to sing. When not working, I shut work from my mind.

— Interview in *The Bookman,* 1921

LOUISA MAY ALCOTT:
"BUT TWO HOURS A DAY"

 I used to write from morning till night without fatigue when "the steam was up." Now, however, I am paying the penalty of twenty years of over work, & can write but two hours a day, doing about twenty pages, sometimes more, though my right thumb is useless from writer's cramp.

— From a letter to journalist Frank Carpenter, 1887

L.M. Montgomery: Solitude not required

 I have had a hard time trying to arrange for enough spare minutes to do some writing. As my salary only suffices for board and bed and as it is against the law, not to mention the climate, to go about naked, I have to make enough money to clothe myself in other ways. My first idea was to write in the evenings. Well, I tried it. I couldn't string two marketable ideas together. Besides, I had to keep my stockings darned and my buttons sewed on!

Then I determined to get up at six every morning to write before going to work! I did that twice — or maybe it was three times. Then I concluded that was impossible. I could not do good work in a chilly room on an empty stomach, especially if, as was often the case, I had been up late the night before. So I said to myself, very solemnly, "Now, Maud, what are you going to do? You have to choose between two courses. You must either decamp back to the tight little Island or you must hit upon some plan to make possible the production of pot-boilers."

Now, it used to be at home that I thought undisturbed solitude was necessary that the fire of genius might burn. I must be alone and the room must be quiet. It would have been the last thing to enter my imagination to suppose that I could ever write anything at all, much less anything of value, in a newspaper office, with rolls of proof shooting down every few minutes, people coming and going and conversing, telephones ringing and machines thumping and dragging overhead. I would have laughed at the idea — yea, I would have laughed it to scorn. But the impossible has happened. I am of one opinion with the Irishman who said you could get used to anything, even to being hanged!

Every morning here I write and not bad stuff either. I have grown accustomed to stopping in the midst of a paragraph to interview a prowling caller and to pausing in full career after an elusive rhyme to read a batch of proof and snarled-up copy. It's all in a day's work — but I don't like it over and above. It's trying. However, it has to be done and I won't grumble, no, not one little bit!

— From her journal, entry dated January 1910

WHO AMONG US TIME-CRUNCHED WORDSMITHS CAN'T OCCASIONALLY relate to Montgomery's wistful longing for "enough spare minutes to do some writing"? This she wrote as a young woman needing to earn her keep, before the novels that would make her a small fortune were published.

Montgomery quickly discovered that the equation of spare time plus perfect solitude was neither practical nor feasible for her. So when she learned to snatch writing time in the midst of a hectic newspaper office, she was surprised at what she could accomplish. She made a habit of writing in less-than-ideal conditions, which served her in good stead throughout her writing life. For her, time and solitude were ever at a premium, and inner peace was nearly nonexistent.

Sarah Orne Jewett wrote to Willa Cather: "To work in silence and with all one's heart, that is the writer's lot; [she] is the only artist who must be solitary, and yet needs the widest outlook upon the world." For most of us, quiet writing time practiced in complete, sweet solitude is a luxury, and a pipe dream if precluded by present circumstances.

Might it be easier to find the time and place to write if total solitude isn't necessarily the ideal to aspire to? What if a bit of hubbub is more conducive? Ironically, now that circumstances allow me to enjoy perfect, rapt silence, I actually get more done when I work with my writing partner, a novelist, at one of the cafés we frequent. Doing so brings me such great focus and efficiency that I believe it was her presence, and our café get-togethers, that were instrumental in helping me to complete this book. A not-entirely-quiet place with just enough background noise might be just what's needed so that "the fire of genius might burn," as Montgomery described it (no doubt with her tongue as firmly in cheek as is mine). In my case, at least, it's a winning formula — with strong caffeine added for good measure.

I TRIED TO WIGGLE OUT OF COVERING THE PAINFUL TOPIC OF WRITER'S block, but my conscience (and editor) wouldn't let me. Honestly, it's almost as if I'm blocked about this subject altogether. Conventional wisdom on what to do when you've hit that proverbial wall is about as much fun as the malady. For example, "try thinking of writing as a job," or "set deadlines and keep them" are two common ideas for unblocking. The first one is about as inspiring as doing laundry (especially for writers who already have a job); and if you could set and keep deadlines, then you wouldn't be blocked in the first place, would you? Learning how to deal with blocks is a critical component of the writer's toolbox, though, so here's a brief survey of what writing women, past and present, have had to say on the subject.

Edna Ferber blamed writer's block on "trying to write better than you can" — referring to the self-consciousness that causes you to seize up and shut down. Anna Quindlen echoed this sentiment in her well-known quote, "People have writer's block not because they can't write, but because they despair of writing eloquently." The answer to this is to be where you are with your writing, and not try to write as the Pulitzer Prize-winning fantasy version of yourself. There's no way to reach soaring heights without taking all the tiny steps to get there. And besides, if you keep your eye on the destination and ignore the journey, you may never get anywhere at all.

Another cause of block is that the proverbial well has run dry. This usually occurs after an intense outpouring of creative effort. Suddenly, there's nothing left, not a drop to squeeze from your previously productive mind. The solution to this depletion, wisely recommended by creativity coaches like Julia Cameron and others, is to pause and let the well fill up again, indulging in outings, adventures, social and cultural experiences, and other inspiring (or restful) pleasures. Sylvia Plath recognized the need for refueling, writing in a letter, "If I have a dry spell ... I wait and live harder, eyes, ears, and heart open, and when the productive time comes, it is that much richer."

Procrastination, self-sabotage, and unnecessary distractions aren't necessarily causes of block, but contribute to feelings of helplessness in mitigating it. Often, the root can be ambiguous, so finding a specific remedy is tricky. As with physical health, one of the ways many writers have dealt with block is prevention. Just as you keep your body limber with exercise, you can keep your writer's mind agile simply by continuing to write, whatever form it might take, most every day. Many writers of the past produced a copious literary output, and were also vigorous letter-writers (Virginia Woolf and George Sand come immediately to mind). Few people write long letters any more, so detailed, effusive e-mails or blog posts might stand in for epistolary writing practice.

In the classic guide *If You Want to Write* (1938), Brenda Ueland posits that blocks come from focusing too much on the big picture, so that "when you plan such a huge edifice of words, your heart fails you." She urged all writers to "keep a slovenly, headlong, impulsive, honest diary," as a way to "discover that the ideas in you are an inexhaustible fountain." Keeping a diary or journal (I use the terms synonymously here), though not a revolutionary idea, has long been a favorite tool to keep words flowing, whether in service of recording daily events, capturing ideas, or venting. For L.M. Montgomery, her journal was a trusted friend that served all these purposes. Madeleine L'Engle touted journal-keeping for similar ends: "A journal is a place where you can unload, dump, let go. It is, among other practical things, a safety valve ... And it's where I jot down ideas for stories, descriptions of a face seen on a subway, a sunset seen over the Hudson, or our Litchfield Hills."

Maya Angelou wrote, "I make writing as much a part of my life as I do eating or listening to music." So it's not surprising that she has also recommended writing regularly, even if you're blocked or simply uninspired, and even if it begins as twaddle: "I may write for two weeks 'the cat sat on the mat, that is that, not a rat.' And it might be just the most boring and awful stuff ... And then it's as if the muse is convinced that I'm serious and says, 'Okay. Okay. I'll come.'"

CHAPTER FOUR | Conquering Inner Demons

Outwardly, what is simpler than to write books? Outwardly, what obstacles are there for a woman rather than for a man? Inwardly, I think, the case is very different. She has still many ghosts to fight, many prejudices to overcome. Indeed it will be a long time still, I think, before a woman can sit down to write a book without finding a phantom to be slain, a rock to be dashed against.

— Virginia Woolf,
   "Professions for Women"
   (essay), 1931

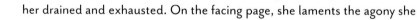

"Writing is agony," proclaimed Edna Ferber. And she wasn't the only one who felt this way. With a few exceptions, the Literary Ladies (and plenty of other classic authors) experienced the writing life as an arduous journey filled with pitfalls and uncertainty. Here we'll witness encounters with all-too-familiar demons. Aside from the agonies of the writing process itself, fear of failure sits on one shoulder while the inner critic taunts from the other.

Margaret Mitchell (1900–1949) speaks for many writers, aspiring or published, when describing her tribulations in writing *Gone with the Wind:* "I had believed that established writers, writers who really knew how to write, had no difficulty at all in writing. I had thought that only luckless beginners like myself had to rewrite endlessly, tear up and throw away whole chapters, start afresh, rewrite and throw away again. I knew nothing about other writers and their working habits, and I thought I was the only writer in the world who went through such goings-on."

In a diary passage, Virginia Woolf describes her mind as "ferociously active." Not content to generalize the writing process from one project to the next, she set the bar not only at different levels but various angles for her books, each becoming its own experiment with form, language, consciousness, and emotion. Every work was meticulously drafted, rewritten, and revised in keeping with her perfectionist tendencies. "I assure you, all my novels were first-rate before they were written," she wrote to Vita Sackville-West in 1928. Crafting a narrative was exhilarating, but the process also left

her drained and exhausted. On the facing page, she laments the agony she put herself through in writing *The Years.* Yet once the very same title that made her vow never to write a long book again topped the U.S. bestseller list, she began dreaming up her next long book.

Though few writers can hold a candle to Woolf's genius, most everyone knows what it's like to curse a work in progress, vowing never to go through such hell again. Witnessing the struggles of those as accomplished as Woolf is a reminder that no matter where we are on the journey, we're not immune from banging our heads against the desk in despair from time to time. Despite such travails, great satisfaction comes from climbing back from the abyss and seeing challenging works come to fruition.

VIRGINIA WOOLF: THE AGONY OF WRITING

 I wonder if anyone has ever suffered so much from a book as I have from *The Years.* Once out I will never look at it again. It's like a long childbirth. Think of that summer, every morning a headache, and forcing myself into that room in my nightgown; and lying down after a page: and always with the certainty of failure. Now that certainty is mercifully removed to some extent. But now I feel I don't care what anyone says so long as I'm rid of it. And for some reason I feel I'm respected and liked. But this is only the haze dance of illusion, always changing. Never write a long book again. Yet I feel I shall write more fiction — scenes will form. But I am tired this morning: too much strain and racing yesterday.

— *A Writer's Diary*, entry dated November 9, 1936

...AND THE ECSTASY

 Did I say ... that Brace* wrote and said they were happy to find that *The Years* is the bestselling novel in America? This was confirmed by my place at the head of the list in the *Herald Tribune*. They have sold 25,000 — my record, easily. (Now I am dreaming of *Three Guineas.*)

— *A Writer's Diary*, entry dated June 14, 1937
  *Referring to her publisher, Harcourt, Brace & Co.

Is the time coming when I can endure to read my own writing in print without blushing — shivering and wishing to take cover?

— Virginia Woolf,
A Writer's Diary, entry
dated March, 1919

 It is worth mentioning, for future reference, that the creative power which bubbles so pleasantly in beginning a new book quiets down after a time, and one goes on more steadily. Doubts creep in. Then one becomes resigned. Determination not to give in, and the sense of an impending shape keep one at it more than anything. I'm a little anxious. How am I to bring off this conception? Directly one gets to work is like a person walking, who has seen the country stretching out before. I want to write nothing in this book that I don't enjoy writing. Yet writing is always difficult.

— *A Writer's Diary,* entry dated May 11, 1920

THE ILLUSION OF GOOD WRITING

*My proofs** come every other day and* I could depress myself adequately if I went into that. The thing now reads thin and pointless; the words scarcely dint the paper; and I expect to be told I've written a graceful fantasy, without much bearing upon real life. Can one tell? Anyhow, nature obligingly supplies me with the illusion that I am about to write something good; something rich and deep and fluent, and hard as nails, while bright as diamonds.

— *A Writer's Diary,* entry dated May 1st, 1927
* Referring to *Jacob's Room*

DESPITE (OR BECAUSE OF) HER BRILLIANCE, VIRGINIA WOOLF WAS continually beset with self-doubt. It's now widely believed that she suffered from bipolar disorder. There were scant options for treatment at that time, and so, during particularly bad bouts of mania or depression, she withdrew, unable to participate in her active social life, and found it nearly impossible to focus on writing. In *The Marriage of Heaven and Hell: Manic Depression and the Life of Virginia Woolf,* author and psychiatrist Peter Dally writes: "Virginia's need to write was, among other things, to make sense out of mental chaos and gain control of madness. Through her novels she made her inner world less frightening. Writing was often agony but it provided the 'strongest pleasure' she knew." Dally discerned a pattern by which Woolf appeared excited yet stable when starting a new book; then, when shaping and revising, her mood gave way to exhaustion and depression.

She referred to herself as "mad," experiencing hallucinatory voices and visions that hinted at mental illness even above and beyond the cyclical manias and depressions. "My own brain is to me the most unaccountable of machinery — always buzzing, humming, soaring roaring diving, and then buried in mud," she wrote in a 1932 letter. "And why? What's this passion for?"

Leonard Woolf was ever vigilant of his wife's mental state; he cared for and protected her as best as anyone could. This was clearly a marriage of minds, if not a typical union, and there is little doubt that he helped create the best possible scenario for her writing life, given the circumstances. As is well known, Virginia Woolf's inner demons got the best of her, and she succumbed to suicide in 1941, at the age of fifty-nine.

Some time after his wife's death, Leonard Woolf edited her diaries, which offer one of the most intimate glimpses available of the creative process at its finest, despite soaring highs and crashing lows. An edited version of the five-volume diaries, *A Writer's Diary,* can serve as a bedside companion to anyone who wishes to witness the unfolding of genius. Eudora Welty was but one writer who felt her influence: "Any day you open it to will be tragic, and yet all the marvelous things she says about her work, about working, leave you filled with joy that's stronger than your misery for her. Remember — 'I'm not very far along, but I think I have my statues against the sky'? Isn't that beautiful?"

IN A 1928 LETTER TO VIRGINIA WOOLF, VITA Sackville-West, the British author, pondered, "Is it better to be extremely ambitious, or rather modest? Probably the latter is safer; but I hate safety, and would rather fail gloriously than dingily succeed." Would that more writers and other artists felt this way! Follow the creative path of anyone accomplished in her field, and you'll likely find that failure isn't the flip side of success, but its occasional companion. Risk can end in either failure or success, but the latter can rarely be achieved without it.

C.S. Lewis was one of the first to set the stage for juvenile fantasy literature, exploring darker themes with *The Chronicles of Narnia,* first published in the early 1950s. However, this didn't seem to smooth the way for Madeleine L'Engle when it came time to submit the now-classic young adult novel *A Wrinkle in Time.* She knew full well what a risk it was to write a book for children that overtly examined good and evil, and though she was crushed each time it was turned down (and it was turned down many, many times), she held fast to her belief in the book.

When risk is avoided, there's less chance of failure, and even less of smashing success. Risk avoidance also prolongs lingering in one's comfort zone — which can be quite cozy, but in the end can feel constraining. I've often wondered: what if I'd been less invested in constructing a safe and somewhat predictable creative life? What will I do with all the notebooks that are filled with wild and fanciful ideas, and a smaller window of time to pursue them? For starters, I'm going to heed Madeleine L'Engle's words of advice. Risk is scary and uncomfortable, but there can be no growth, and little glory, without it.

MADELEINE L'ENGLE: RISKING FAILURE

 Risk is essential. It's scary. Every time I sit down and start the first page of a novel I am risking failure. We are encouraged in this world not to fail. College students are often encouraged to take the courses they are going to get A's in so that they can get that nice grant to graduate school. And they are discouraged from taking the courses they may not get a good grade in but which fascinate them nevertheless. I think that is a bad thing that the world has done to us.

We are encouraged only to do that which we can be successful in. But things are accomplished only by our risk of failure. Writers will never do anything beyond the first thing unless they risk growing.

— *Madeleine L'Engle Herself*, 2001

FAILURE IS NO PICNIC, NOR THE FEAR OF IT, BUT the prospect of success can be just as scary. Actually, in some ways success can be scarier. It shakes up the status quo; failure is more likely to maintain it — you can continue to dance with the devil you know.

I wonder whether Margaret Mitchell had another book in her after the mega-success of *Gone with the Wind*. She was only forty-eight when a motorist struck and killed her, but still, that occurred twelve years after the publication of her blockbuster. And Harper Lee, author of *To Kill a Mockingbird*, seemed a bit rattled by her first (and as it turned out, only) book's success: "I never expected any sort of success with *Mockingbird*. I didn't expect the book to sell in the first place. I was hoping for a quick and merciful death at the hands of reviewers, but at the same time I sort of hoped that maybe someone would like it enough to give me encouragement … I got rather a whole lot, and in some ways this was just about as frightening as the quick, merciful death I'd expected." It's as if their success was so excessive that it led to a kind of paralysis.

Like Edna Ferber, it's possible to view success and failure as parts of an intertwined process rather than as polar opposites. If you fail once in a while, it means you're stretching beyond your comfort zone. Also, your view of success won't always match with the world's. I've done projects I considered smashingly successful in terms of creative effort and enjoyment that have fallen like lead balloons, while others I've deemed ho-hum continue to put food on the table years after publication. Since preconceived notions of success can be as immobilizing as the fear of failure, neither should have a place at the desk when you're sitting down to work. Do as Edna Ferber would, and don't invite them.

There is the danger, always, of trying to write better than you can. The next book, the one you are just beginning to cope with, must be better than the one before it, or before that, you say (but not consciously). It must be more seriously conceived, more entertaining, more adult; fresher, more vital. This naturally brings up a hideous structure known in writers' psychological language as a block, and as a result you can't write anything.

— Edna Ferber
A Kind of Magic, 1963

EDNA FERBER: "SUCCESS OR FAILURE, ALL'S TO DO AGAIN"

 In the working-day life of a professional writer success or failure is very likely to sum up much the same at the end. I don't mean that failure is as pleasant as success. I've known both. Success stimulates the glands, revivifies the spirits, feeds the ego, fills the purse. Failure is a depressing thing to face. The critics rip your play to ribbons, audiences refuse to come to it; reviewers say your book is dull, or trite, readers will not buy it. You read these things, you hear them, you face them as you would face any misfortune, with as much good grace as you can summon.

Success or failure, you go on to the next piece of work at hand. There may be a day of brooding or sulking or self-pity or resentment. But next morning there's coffee and the newspaper and your typewriter, and the world. What's done is done. Win or lose, success or failure, all's to do again. If a lawyer or a doctor or a merchant or an engineer fails at a task it is, usually, a matter of private concern. But the failure of a playwright, an actor, a novelist, a musician, is publicly and scathingly announced and broadcast and published over an entire continent and frequently the whole civilized world. Often the terms of that announcement are cruel, personal, or even malicious, though this last is rare. Yet next day or next week, there [she] is, writing, acting, singing, or playing again. That's being a craftsman.

— *A Peculiar Treasure,* 1939

GEORGE SAND:
WRITING IS HARD; SELF-PITY IS EASIER

 As for my frenzy for work, I will compare it to an attack of Herpes. I scratch myself while I cry. It is both a pleasure and a torture at the same time. And I am doing nothing that I want to! For one does not choose one's subjects, they force themselves on one. Shall I ever find mine? Will an idea fall from Heaven suitable to my temperament? Can I write a book to which I shall give myself heart and soul? It seems to me in my moments of vanity, that I am beginning to catch a glimpse of what a novel ought to be. But I still have three or four of them to write before that one (which is, moreover, very vague), and at the rate I am going, if I write these three or four, that will be the most I can do.

— From a letter to Gustave Flaubert, 1866

GEORGE SAND MADE A HABIT OF ASKING TO be pitied for her literary agonies. Despite her complaints, the word "prolific" is woefully inadequate to describe her output. Aside from the literary accomplishments detailed on page 22, she also wielded a journalistic pen to give voice to her concerns for women's rights and social justice. She started her own newspaper right around the time of the revolution of 1848 to disseminate her progressive and socialist views. One of the earliest and best-known cross-dressers, she wore men's clothing both for comfort (for traveling, which she loved — apparently trousers were more practical than crinolines) and to make a statement. Similarly, she was famed (and mocked) for her public cigar-smoking, and never went far without her beloved hookah.

To her critics, Sand responded, "The world will know and understand me someday. But if that day does not arrive, it does not greatly matter. I shall have opened the way for other women." Given that she was nothing short of a force of nature, did the lady protest too much?

If someone like George Sand needed to *kvetch* so regularly, there must be something to be said for externalizing one's mental dross, whether to a writing group or a Flaubert-type colleague. And by the way, Flaubert gave as good as he got, whining to Sand about his creative woes, "I feel like weeping at times. You ought to pity me!" So unless you're willing to listen as well as unload, a private journal might be the better bet for spilling your troubles. And bear in mind this bit of wisdom from Maya Angelou: "Self-pity in its early stages is as snug as a feather mattress. Only when it hardens does it become uncomfortable."

I think I may boast myself to be, with all possible Vanity, the most unlearned, & uninformed Female who ever dared to be an Authoress.

— Jane Austen
From a letter to James
Stanier, 1815

IN BOOKS ABOUT THE WRITING PROCESS, MUCH ink has been spilled in protest against the "inner critic." This dreadful demon is most often described as the voice in your head convincing you that you're unworthy, that you have no idea what you're doing, and above all, that you're a delusional fraud. But this chapter offers ample proof that some of the greatest minds in literature had noisy inner critics.

Of course, you don't want the voice in your head to insult and berate, but what if it's there to keep you from becoming complacent, to drive you to achieve more, and to keep you humble? Colette claimed that the writer who loses her self-doubt "should stop writing immediately," and lay aside her pen. Perhaps the inner critic would have a better reputation and a more useful function if we thought of it not as an adversary, but as a loving friend or wise editor who's honest enough to say, "This is good. But I know you can do even better."

JANE AUSTEN: HER INNER CRITIC SPEAKS

The work* is rather too light and bright and sparkling; it wants shade; it wants to be stretched out here and there with a long chapter — of senses if it could be had; if not, of solemn specious nonsense — about something unconnected with the story; an essay on writing, a critique on Walter Scott, or the history of Buonoparté, or anything that would form a contrast, and bring the reader with increased delight to the playfulness and epigrammatism of the general style.

— From a letter to her sister Cassandra, 1813
   *Referring to *Pride and Prejudice*

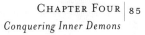

I can work indefatigably at the correction of a work before it leaves my hands, but when once I have looked on it as completed and submitted to the inspection of others, it becomes next to impossible to alter or amend. With the heavy suspicion on my mind that all may not be right, I yet feel forced to put up with the inevitably wrong.

— Charlotte Brontë
  From a letter to W. S. Williams
  (her editor), 1849

Anaïs Nin: "I write in a scattering fashion"

 When I look down upon my work, it shrinks to almost nothing. One day I write poems and essays, and the next I tear and burn them, to begin again, and in the same manner I have done this for years. Nothing satisfies me. The reading I do serves only to impress me with my inferiority of style and character. I write in a scattering fashion, always with a purpose in mind and yet never capable of reaching it. My work lacks "roundness," concentration, and clearness. I drift into vague visions and abstract forms and above all into superfluities. Although it is not so, it appears very much as if my mind wandered; when I most want to appear fixed upon my subject, I deviate and I miss my point, and above all what I cannot forgive myself is the unreliableness of my judgment because of my enthusiasm.

Against all these handicaps, I have only a few remedies. I know that I have application, a hard-headed kind of persistence. Where will all this lead me? Roundness, concentration, and clearness can be acquired. Directness and the eloquent virtue of reserve equally so. I maintain they are the infirmities of my age, and I will not always be eighteen. Probably in a year or so I will have exhausted these powers and a period of quiet will follow, a period of settled judgment, of moderate opinions, a more judicious reasoning, and instead of jumping to conclusions, I will arrive at them. . .

Nevertheless, I am resolved to write, write, and write. Nothing can turn me away from a path I have definitely set myself to follow.

— *The Early Diaries of Anaïs Nin,*
   Entry dated 1921

EDITH WHARTON: EMERGING FROM SELF-DOUBT

 I have often wondered, in looking back at the slow stammering beginnings of my literary life, whether or not it is a good thing for the creative artist to grow up in an atmosphere where the arts are simply nonexistent. Violent opposition might be a stimulous — but was it helpful or the reverse to have every aspiration ignored, or looked at askance? I have thought over this many times, as I have over most problems of creative art, in the fascinating but probably idle attempt to discover how it is all done, and exactly what happens at that "fine point of the soul" where the creative act, like the mystic's union with the Unknowable, really seems to take place.

And as I have grown older my point of view has necessarily changed, since I have seen more and more would-be creators, whether in painting, music, or letters, whose way has been made smooth from the cradle, geniuses whose families were prostrate before them before they had written a line or composed a measure, and who, in middle age, still sat in ineffectual ecstasy before the blank page or the empty canvas; while on the other hand, more and more of the baffled, the derided, or the ignored have fought their way to achievement...as regards a case like my own, where a development no doubt naturally slow was certainly retarded by the indifference of every one about me, it is hard to say whether or not I was hindered. I am inclined to think the drawbacks were outweighed by the advantages; chief among these being the fact that I escaped all premature flattery, all local celebrity, that I had to fight my way to expression through a thick fog of indifference, if not tacit disapproval, and that when at last I met one of two kindred minds their criticisms were to me as sharp and searching as if they had been professionals in the exercise of their calling.

— *A Backward Glance,* 1934

FROM MUCH ANECDOTAL EVIDENCE, IT APPEARS that women suffer from the "impostor syndrome" with more frequency than do men. Even among high achievers, there's a fairly common belief that personal success has more to do with luck, timing, or external circumstances rather than with talent. If it's any comfort, the book *If I'm So Successful, Why Do I Feel Like a Fake?* by Joan Harvey and Cynthia Katz, presents research demonstrating that accomplished people often feel like frauds. Even after the success of her book, *The Yearling,* Marjorie Kinnan Rawlings voiced a familiar attitude when she wrote, "I feel that I have no pretensions to artistry, that I have my bally nerve ever to sit down to the typewriter again." Perhaps some measured appreciation for success is preferable to allowing your ego to run amok. Still, there's no clear benefit to being overly humble or taking no credit at all for one's own accomplishments.

Edith Wharton struggled to feel worthy of her right to write, let alone to deserve any sort of achievement at this vocation. No haughty heiress, she felt inferior to the writers of her time that she longed to have as peers, fearing they wouldn't take her seriously. She tiptoed into the publishing field by producing *The Decoration of Houses* and *Italian Villas and Their Gardens* before gathering enough courage to try her hand at poetry and short stories. Her successful efforts at nonfiction led her to just the right contacts for this pursuit. She was pleasantly surprised at how quickly she got her foot in the door — and at how well her work was received.

It expresses a healthy attitude on her part that she deemed lack of early support as somehow a good thing — forcing her to fight her way out of the "thick fog of indifference." A less intrepid soul may have stayed mired in the self-limiting beliefs imposed by family and heedless cohorts.

After all, one knows one's weak points so well, that it's rather bewildering to have the critics overlook them & invent others.

— Edith Wharton
  From a letter, 1907

CHAPTER FIVE | *The Writer Mother*

*O*ur children are just coming
to the age when everything
depends on my efforts. They
are delicate in health, and
nervous and excitable and need
a mother's whole attention. Can
I lawfully divide my attention by
literary efforts?

— Harriet Beecher Stowe
   From a letter to her
   husband, 1841

THERE HAVE BEEN MANY DAYS WHEN THE DEMANDS OF FAMILY LIFE have overwhelmed my need and desire to work. I know I'm not alone. When I hear gripes from my writing and art cohorts (in traditional relationships) about laundry or household chores or men's amazing ability not to see messes, I'm pretty confident that it's not really about the socks on the floor or the dishes in the sink. It's that Daddy gets to do his work without thinking about everything and everyone else. And he gets to do it without guilt — which is compounded if your work is actually something you like and gives you creative gratification.

Fewer than half of well-known women authors of the past were mothers, no matter the era in which they lived. Of the dozen authors I focus on in this book, only four were mothers (Stowe, L'Engle, Montgomery, and Sand), and that's a pretty accurate reflection of how the profession looked in the past. In *Silences*, Tillie Olsen listed all notable literary women (in the English-speaking world) and concluded that "until very recently all distinguished achievement has come from childless women." Of course, this has changed since that book was first published in 1978. In the past, childlessness was sometimes a conscious choice; in other cases it was due to circumstances. Virginia Woolf, for instance, wasn't childless by choice; she envied the joy her sister Vanessa Bell derived from her three children. One could speculate on a number of reasons women authors avoided family life. Unstable marriages were commonplace among the literati. Perhaps some were fulfilled enough by the creative life, and didn't feel that they could work with children underfoot. For others, nontraditional relationships and orientations may not have been conducive to family life given cultural attitudes of the past.

Even if they weren't themselves mothers, several of the Literary Ladies (Woolf, Cather, Alcott, and Nin) nevertheless had something to say about children, family life, and choices. Though not entirely dispassionate on the subject, their objective viewpoints are astute. Today, women are freer from the societal imperative to bear children, but I suspect that more women writers than ever do choose to have them. Though it's never easy, it's good to know that women can rock the cradle with one hand and rock the world with the other.

VIRGINIA WOOLF: MUCH DEPENDS ON THE "ORDINARY WOMAN"

The extraordinary woman depends on the ordinary woman. It is only when we know what were the conditions of the average woman's life — the number of her children, whether she had money of her own, if she had a room to herself, whether she had help in bringing up her family, if she had servants, whether part of the housework was her task — it is only when we can measure the way of life and experience made possible to the ordinary woman that we can account for the success or failure of the extraordinary woman as a writer.

— "Women and Fiction" (essay), 1929

To be 29 & unmarried — to be a failure — childless — insane, too, no writer... Why is life so tragic; so like a little strip of pavement over an abyss?...It's having no children, living away from friends, failing to write well.

— Virginia Woolf
   From a letter to
   her sister
   (Vanessa Bell), 1911

WILLA CATHER: HAVING IT ALL

As for the choice between a woman's home and her career, is there any reason why she cannot have both? In France the business is regarded as a family affair. It is taken for granted that Madame will be the business partner of her husband; his bookkeeper, cashier or whatever she fits best. Yet the French women are famous housekeepers and their children do not suffer for lack of care.

The situation is similar if the woman's business is art. Her family life will be a help rather than a hindrance to her; and if she has a quarter of the vitality of her prototype on the farm she will be able to fulfill the claims of both.

— Interview, *Lincoln Daily Star*, 1921

Madeleine L'Engle: On birthing babies and books

 I have a friend, a beautiful and talented young woman, who is afraid to have a child and who is afraid to use her talent to write. She does not yet understand the joy that follows the pain of birth. I've experienced the pain and joy of the birth of babies and the birth of books and there's nothing like it: when a child who has been conceived in love is born to a man and woman, the joy of that birth sings throughout the universe.

— *A Circle of Quiet*, 1972

A better mother when working

 I'm often asked how my children feel about my work, and I have to reply, "ambivalent." Our first-born observed to me many years ago, when she was a grade school child, "Nobody else's mother writes books." But she also said, around the same time, "Mother, you've been very cross and edgy with us lately, and we've noticed that you haven't been writing and we wish you'd get back to the typewriter." A wonderfully freeing remark. I had to learn that I was a better mother and wife when I was working than when I was not.

— *Walking on Water*, 1980

IT'S NO WONDER THE WRITING PROCESS HAS BEEN COMPARED WITH childbirth. Even authors who didn't go through the process themselves appropriated the metaphor. Witness Virginia Woolf on page 75; Edna Ferber said that writing is "a combination of ditch-digging, mountain-climbing, treadmill, and childbirth."

Harriet Beecher Stowe (who knew well the rigors of childbirth) wrote, "Creating a story is like bearing a child and it leaves me in a state as weak and helpless as when my baby was born." Madeleine L'Engle was familiar with the bliss that follows both birthing a baby and birthing a book, once the pain of each subsides.

Each publishing experience, major or minor, can be savored in its own right, though none will ever have the intensity of the first, just like that of a first baby. Then, like having a second or third child, you learn to relax a bit with each publication. I remember how my first book replaced the sun as the object that everything else needed to revolve around. Fortunately, each subsequent publication has become more like a piece of an expanding quilt, a separate component that connects with others to become part of a body of work.

Harriet Beecher Stowe:
A room of her own

 If I am to write, I must have a room to myself, which shall be my room ... All last winter I felt the need of some place where I could go and be quiet and satisfied. I could not there [in the dining room], for there was all the setting of tables, and clearing up of tables, and dressing and washing of children, and everything else going on, and the continual falling of soot and coal dust on everything in the room was a constant annoyance to me, and I never felt comfortable there, though I tried hard. Then if I came into the parlor where you were, I felt as if I were interrupting you, and you know you sometimes thought so, too.

Now this winter let the cooking stove be put into that room, and let the pipe run up through the floor into the room above ... You can study by the parlor fire, and I and my plants will take the other room. I shall keep my work and all my things there and feel settled and quiet. I intend to have a regular part of each day devoted to the children, and then I shall take them in there.

— From a letter to her husband, 1841

HARRIET BEECHER STOWE, AS WE'VE LEARNED, WAS A HARD-WORKING writer as her brood of children grew up. Her husband was a firm supporter of her talents, but was no help in the household, and not much of a provider. Struggling with divided loyalties, her assertion to her husband in this letter, "If I am to write, I must have a room to myself" neatly presages Virginia Woolf's avowal that "a woman must have money and a room of her own if she is to write fiction."

However much Stowe longed for money and privacy, it could be argued that being a mother played a pivotal role in the inception of her magnum opus, *Uncle Tom's Cabin*. When she lost her beloved son, Samuel Charles, to cholera at age eighteen months, the grief was crushing. Later, she claimed that this loss helped her empathize with slave mothers whose children were torn from them to be auctioned off: "I wrote what I did because as a woman, as a mother, I was oppressed and broken-hearted with the sorrows and injustice I saw."

The book Stowe longed to write "to make this whole nation feel what an accursed thing slavery is" was put off from one year to the next: "As long as the baby sleeps with me nights I can't do much at anything, but I will do it at last." At age thirty-nine, still in the midst of tending to her large family, Stowe found a way to disseminate the story she longed to tell, publishing monthly installments in an abolitionist newsletter. With each issue, public interest built. At the same time, she wrote sketches for various publications like *Godey's Lady's Book* (which likely were more lucrative outlets). Stowe decided, despite the slim household budget, to devote "about three hours per day in writing ... I have determined not to be a mere domestic slave ... I mean to have money enough to have my house kept in the best manner and yet to have time for reflection and preparation for the education of my children which every mother needs."

In *Silences*, Tillie Olsen detailed the sacrifices women writers have historically made (compromising both literary achievement and a full family life). She argues that certain writers like Stowe were able to pursue their literary goals because they "had servants." Nonsense. Stowe hired help with her own hard-earned money because she understood the value of her own time. She had precious little time and money, and evidently took care to spend both wisely.

I WISH I HAD KNOWN ABOUT HARRIET BEECHER STOWE'S LIFE WHEN my sons were growing up. Her experiences put the usual gamut of mom-ish complaints into perspective. Not enough sleep, lack of time and privacy, and run-of-the-mill household chaos pale in comparison to the circumstances in which she composed her stories and novels. Though she produced a good share of the household income, Stowe was solely in charge of the domestic duties and children, as were all women of her time. Writing was done in the midst of vast responsibilities and intermittent grief, having lost three of her seven children in various ways.

In *Silences,* cited on the previous page, Tillie Olsen details the price she herself paid for putting writing on hold while raising four children: "The habits of a lifetime when everything else had to come before writing are not easily broken, even when circumstances now often make it possible for writing to be first; habits of years — response to others, distractibility for daily matters — stay with you, become you. The cost of 'discontinuity' (that pattern still imposed on women) is such a weight of things unsaid, an accumulation of material so great, that everything starts up something else in me; what should take weeks, takes me sometimes months to write; what should take months, takes years."

Compelled to write for a living, Stowe didn't have the option of discontinuity. Staying in the habit served her well once the time was finally right to begin the work she believed she was meant to produce. The four Literary Ladies who were mothers had one thing in common — they never stopped writing. They demonstrated how it can be done in the crevices of a chaotic life — plots hatched and developed while attending to other duties; a few hours of writing snatched while children are otherwise occupied or cared for. Writing when conditions are less than ideal is incredibly difficult. But looking at the lives of writers that seemed more idyllic, it appears there's no such thing as "ideal." Stowe's journey conveyed that while it's never going to be easy, if there are words you want to commit to paper, find incremental ways to do so, rather than waiting for that elusive "some day." Even if it doesn't turn out to be the grand-scale, full-blown masterpiece you may envision, it's good to make even a modest beginning. For many of us, "some day" has already arrived.

Harriet Beecher Stowe: Interruptions ...

We have had terrible weather here ... The cold has been so intense that the children have kept begging to get up from table at meal-times to warm feet and fingers. Our airtight stoves warm all but the floor — heat your head and keep your feet freezing. If I sit by the open fire in the parlor my back freezes, if I sit in my bedroom and try to write my head aches and my feet are cold...

When I have a headache and feel sick, as I do to-day, there is actually not a place in the house where I can lie down and take a nap without being disturbed. Overhead is the school-room, next door is the dining-room, and the girls practice there two hours a day. If I lock my door and lie down some one is sure to be rattling the latch before fifteen minutes have passed...

— From a letter to her husband, 1850

... AND MORE INTERRUPTIONS

Since I began this note I have been called off at least a dozen times — once for the fish-man, to buy a codfish — once to see a man who had brought me some baskets of apples — once to see a book man ... then to nurse the baby — then into the kitchen to make a chowder for dinner and now I am at it again for nothing but deadly determination enables me to ever write — it is rowing against wind and tide.

— From a letter to her
  sister-in-law, 1850

Self–abnegation is a noble thing but I think there is a limit to it, & though in a few rare cases it may work well yet half the misery of the world seems to come from unmated pairs trying to live their lie decorously to the end, & bringing children into the world to inherit the unhappiness & discord out of which they were born.

— Louisa May Alcott
  From a letter to a friend, 1865

LOUISA MAY ALCOTT WROTE EVOCATIVELY IN HER fiction of childhood, youth, and even motherhood. But through her heroines, she resisted allowing domestic concerns, or even romance to completely define a woman's identity. Some of her heroines, notably Jo March Bhaer of the *Little Women* series, and the title character of *Rose in Bloom,* were embodiments of her own ambition and drive. Clearly, she was ambivalent on the subjects of marriage and motherhood. It's possible that her observation on "unmated pairs trying to live their lie" referred to her own parents. Yet she wrote about her sister Anna, a contented mother, "She is a happy woman! I sell my children [referring to her books], and though they feed me, they don't love me as hers do."

Alarmingly naïve about the nature of her sexuality, Alcott confessed in an 1883 interview: "I am more than half-persuaded that I am a man's soul, put by some freak of nature into a woman's body ... because I have fallen in love in my life with so many pretty girls and never once the least bit with any man." Perhaps unknowingly, the repressed nature of her sexuality helped her avoid the circumscribed path of marriage and motherhood, and allowed her to view the institution more dispassionately.

In the end, Alcott got to have a brief experience with motherhood. Her youngest sister, Amy, while training as an artist in Europe (subsidized by Alcott's earnings), married, had a daughter, and died within a year of giving birth. Alcott wanted to raise the child, and earned the father's family's consent do so. Adopted at the age of two, the little girl was her Aunt Louisa's namesake (and nicknamed Lulu); from all accounts, the nine years they spent together before Alcott's death were happy ones.

ON THE WHOLE, GEORGE SAND WAS AN ADORING MOTHER, BUT FOR her, motherhood was often fraught with the kind of drama that colored many of her relationships prior to mellow older age. Her son, Maurice, was a major mama's boy, causing petty jealousy for Sand's most famed live-in lover, Frédéric Chopin. Could it have been from spite that Chopin fell in love with Sand's daughter, Solange, when she was a pretty and flirtatious young lady of seventeen?

From her grandmother, Sand inherited an exquisite estate in Nohant, located in the Indre region of central France. There she hosted a legion of writers and artists with whom she was friendly, including Delacroix, Turgenev, Flaubert, Liszt, and Balzac. Summers found her retreating to it from hectic city life in Paris. She located to that idyllic locale permanently for her last years.

Aimee McKenzie wrote in her 1921 introduction to *The George Sand–Gustave Flaubert Letters*: "In her final retreat at Nohant, surrounded by her affectionate children and grandchildren, diligently writing, botanizing, bathing in her little river, visited by her friends and undistracted by the fiery lovers of the old time, she shows an unguessed wealth of maternal virtue, swift, comprehending sympathy, fortitude, sunny resignation, and a goodness of heart that has ripened into wisdom."

It's an unexpected revelation that literature's wild woman would settle down to such domestic tranquility in her final years. Much of the pleasure she derived was from having (mostly) healed the tumultuous relationship with her daughter, acquiring a stellar daughter-in-law, and above all, from her granddaughters, who she genuinely adored. Her over-the-top sexuality gave way to a doting maternal nature, and her spendthrift ways to a desire to "have a little to leave to my children and grandchildren."

Part of that "little" she left them included the Nohant estate. Eventually, one of her granddaughters transferred the estate to France to be designated as a National Historic Monument, which is open to visitors.

Even if it seems presumptuous, it's a pleasant flight of fancy to dream of the legacy you might be able to pass along to your loved ones from your literary endeavors. Isn't it wonderful to imagine that something you've created will survive for the next generation to enjoy?

George Sand: "A little to leave to my children"

And now I am very old, gently traversing my sixty-fifth year. By some freak of destiny I am stronger and more active than I was in youth. I can walk farther. I can stay awake longer. My body has remained supple as a glove...I never catch cold, and I have forgotten what rheumatism is. I am absolutely calm. My old age is as chaste in thought as it is in deed. I have no regret for youth, no ambition for fame, and no desire for money, except that I would like to have a little to leave to my children and grandchildren...

I no longer live in myself. My heart has gone into my children and my friends. I suffer only through their sufferings...I care very little about living on. Death is kind and gentle. My only dread of death is in the thought of the grief it would cause my loved ones.

Have I been useful to them these last twenty years? I believe so. I have earnestly wanted to be. So I was wrong when I used to imagine that there are crises in life when one may hand in one's resignation without injury to others. Because here I am, still useful at an advanced age. My brain has not failed. Indeed I feel that it has acquired a great deal and that it is better nourished than it ever was ... Meanwhile, and nevertheless, one approaches the journey's end. But the end is a goal, not a catastrophe.

— "Final Comment by George Sand," (essay) 1868

"THERE ARE ENOUGH WOMEN TO DO THE CHILDBEARING AND THE childrearing. I know of none who can write my books," proclaimed Australian author H. H. Richardson (1870–1946). Katherine Anne Porter concurred: "Now I am all for human life, and I am all for marriage and children and all that sort of thing, but quite often you can't have that and do what you were supposed to do, too." Yet Porter took twenty years to write *Ship of Fools* because she was "trying to get to that table, to that typewriter, away from my jobs of teaching and trooping this country and of keeping house." Keeping house? Some excuse, especially for one opposed to having children.

Porter's philosophical avoidance of childbearing contrasts starkly with what her fellow novelist and short story writer Shirley Jackson (1916–1965) did — she had four children and used them in her fiction and nonfiction: "It is much easier, I find, to write a story than to cope competently with the millions of daily trials and irritations that turn up in an ordinary house, and it helps a good deal — particularly with children around — if you can see them through a flattering veil of fiction. It has always been a comfort to me to make stories out of things that happen, things like moving, and kittens, and Christmas concerts at the grade school, and broken bicycles ... "

Jackson's haunting classic short story, *The Lottery,* first catapulted her to fame in 1948, and her prodigious output (six novels, four children's books, and dozens of short stories) continued apace during the years of childrearing. She also mined family adventures and misadventures for wry, cheery observations in her idealized memoirs, *Life Among the Savages* (1952) and *Raising Demons* (1957). These family stories may well have inspired the genre that Laura Shapiro called "the literature of domestic chaos" later perfected by Erma Bombeck. Echoes of this form reverberate in today's abundance of "momoirs" and motherhood blogs. From her darker side, Stephen King was influenced by her tales of psychological terror, and dedicated his novel, *Firestarter,* "In memory of Shirley Jackson."

L.M. Montgomery was another writing mother who wove personal experiences with marriage and motherhood into her work. Fiction became a buffer against resentment at the roles she maintained, first as a dutiful granddaughter, then as an upstanding minister's wife and devoted mother. Though these weren't entirely facades, her spirited female characters hint at rebellion toward limited roles and opportunities.

Montgomery had two sons, and she reveled in their early childhoods. Parallel to the standard descriptions of her own mental state that forever peppered her journals (listing "sleeplessness," "utter nervous prostration," "dreadful weariness of spirit," "restlessness," and many other such complaints), she cooed over her children. The elder was described as "a big sturdy fellow, full of ebullient energy, a loyal, straightforward little soul, with a very tender heart." About her younger, she wrote that he "has dear, appealing ways and delicious little gurgles of laughter and fun." Between the two boys she experienced a devastating stillbirth and recreated this event in *Anne's House of Dreams,* in which Anne Shirley's first baby is born dead. Subsequently, Anne experiences the joys of motherhood as well as a writing career much like Montgomery's, and a deeply satisfying marriage, unlike the author's.

A subplot in *Anne's House of Dreams* described in *Writing a Life* by Mary Rubio and Elizabeth Waterston, "concerns another woman, trapped in a meaningless marriage: passionate, colorful Leslie Moor is married to a handsome man who through an accident has become a being without mind or personality." Later, she continues, "Leslie is released from her tomb of a marriage." Montgomery herself was not so lucky, trapped in her marriage to Ewan MacDonald. Though his mental state was apparently not from an injury like his fictional counterpart's, their similarities are thinly veiled.

As Montgomery's sons grew, early joys gave way to full-blown anxieties as they drifted through common trials and tribulations of late adolescence and early adulthood. As her own psychological health and personal life deteriorated, her novels and stories became ever more mature and complex. One can only marvel that a mother, wife, and writer who so often confessed such sentiments to her journal as "I have just spent two days in hell," could keep the flame of creation burning so brightly, and so constantly."

ANAïS NIN: "THE UNBROKEN TIE"

 Judy Chicago, the well-known painter and teacher, made a study of women painters and found that, whereas the men painters all had studios separate from the house, the women did not, and painted either in the kitchen or some spare room. But many young women have taken literally Virginia Woolf's *A Room of One's Own* and rented studios away from the family ... The very feeling of "going to work," the physical act of detachment, the sense of value given to the work by isolating it, became a stimulant and a help. To create another life, they found, was not a breaking away or separating. It is striking that for women any break or separation carries with it an aura of loss, as if the symbolic umbilical cord still affected all her emotional life and each act were a threat to unity and ties.

This fear is in women, not in men, but it was learned from men. Men, led by their ambitions, did separate from their families, were less present for the children, were absorbed, submerged by their professions. But this happened to men and does not necessarily have to happen to women. The unbroken tie lies in the feelings. It is not the hours spent with husband or children, but the quality and completeness of the presence. Man is often physically present and mentally preoccupied. Woman is more capable of turning away from her work to give full attention to a weary husband or a child's scratched finger.

— *In Favor of the Sensitive Man and Other Essays,* 1976

ANYONE WHO HAS ATTEMPTED TO WRITE WHILE RAISING CHILDREN will appreciate Anne Tyler's essay "Still Just Writing." This author of numerous novels (*Breathing Lessons, The Accidental Tourist*) details with good humor her bumpy path to becoming a writer when her children were young:

"It seems to me that since I've had children, I've grown richer and deeper. They may have slowed down my writing for a while, but when I did write, I had more of a self to speak from ... After the children started school, I put up the partitions in my mind. I would rush around in the morning braiding their hair, packing their lunches; then the second they were gone I would grow quiet and climb the stairs to my study. Sometimes a child would come home early and I would feel a little tug between the two parts of me; I'd be absent-minded and short-tempered. Then gradually I learned to make the transition more easily. It feels like a sort of string that I tell myself to loosen."

Another prolific contemporary author, Louise Erdrich (*Love Medicine, The Beet Queen*), echoes the sentiments put forth in Tyler's essay. When asked in a Salon.com interview how being a mother changed her as an artist she said, "I find myself emotionally engaged in ways I wouldn't have been otherwise. I wouldn't understand certain things that I'm starting to get now." Erdrich was inspired by Toni Morrison's writings on the subject, adding, "She spoke about being a mother, and she always spoke about it as a great boon to her as a writer."

Having children can inform the practical as well as the emotional tenor of a writing life. In a *Paris Review* interview, Toni Morrison (*Beloved, Sula*) spoke of how her writing schedule was established with young children at home: "Writing before dawn began as a necessity — I had small children when I first began to write and I needed the time before they said, Mama — and that was always around five in the morning ... eventually I realized that I was clearer-headed, more confident, and generally more intelligent in the morning. The habit of getting up early, which I had formed when the children were young, now became my choice."

Though Anaïs Nin wasn't a mother herself, she understood how easy it is to be diverted by everyone else's needs, even for something as minor as a "scratched finger." If you're a mother, on the many days when you feel like you're not getting enough done, you can remind yourself (while careening from one interruption to another) that you are indeed growing richer and deeper.

CHAPTER SIX | *Rejection and Acceptance*

At last I had groped my way through to my vocation, and thereafter I never questioned that story-telling was my job ... I felt like some homeless waif who, after trying for years to take out naturalization papers, and being rejected by every country, has finally acquired a nationality. The Land of Letters was henceforth to be my country and I gloried in my new citizenship.

— Edith Wharton,
  A Backward Glance, 1934

It's hard to separate the rejection of one's work from the rejection of one's self. Your words are tiny chunks of your soul, so their dismissal can feel as if it's you, personally, who has been tossed aside and discarded. Even impersonal rejections, "not right for our list," or "not looking at submissions at this time," have the power to wound, especially if the writer hasn't yet developed a tough hide.

To illustrate what a sore subject this can be, there are numerous Web sites devoted to the topic (just Google "literary rejection"). One such site, now defunct (rejectioncollection.com), featured actual rejection letters posted by their recipients, followed by responses to the question, "How did this letter make you feel?" I was struck by how many said the rejection made them feel angry or frustrated, whether it was phrased impersonally, gently, or even contained some constructive criticism. Offhand remarks by editors drove their recipients to feel "devastated." Even constructive comments caused rejected writers' defenses to go up.

There are plenty of examples, like those in this chapter, of publishers being just plain wrong — sometimes again and again — about books that went on to become classics. But there are certainly many other instances in which writers refuse to take any constructive criticism and cling to the notion that their freshman efforts are brilliant and beyond reproach. This creates a "me versus them" mindset that's never constructive.

Some of the Literary Ladies endured the sting of repeated rejection, while others made the segue from journalism and other forms of paid writing into the world of book publishing with relative ease. Anaïs Nin was unique in this book's group of authors as one who started a press to publish her own work when she couldn't find a publisher to take on her short stories. Unless you go the self-publishing route from the start, rejection is more often than not part of the process of becoming an author.

It becomes apparent through the Literary Ladies' narratives that rejection and acceptance can sometimes be but a hairsbreadth apart. In this chapter we'll also take a look at the most critical form of acceptance of all — self-acceptance. This is the essential ingredient for becoming, in one's own eyes, someone who deserves success as a writer, whatever form that success might take in each individual's journey.

L.M. MONTGOMERY:
"I KNEW I WOULD 'ARRIVE' SOMEDAY"

After leaving Prince of Wales College I taught school for a year in Bideford, Prince Edward Island. I wrote a good deal and learned a good deal, but my stuff came back except from two periodicals the editors of which evidently thought that literature was its own reward, and quite independent of monetary considerations. I often wonder that I did not give up in utter discouragement. At first I used to feel dreadfully hurt when a story or poem over which I had laboured and agonized came back, with one of those icy little rejection slips. Tears of disappointment would come in spite of myself, as I crept away to hide the poor, crimpled manuscript in the depths of my trunk. But after a while I got hardened to it and did not mind. I only set my teeth and said, "I will succeed." I believed in myself and I struggled on alone, in secrecy and silence. I never told my ambitions and efforts and failures to any one. Down, deep down, under all discouragements and rebuff I knew I would "arrive" some day.

— *The Alpine Path,* 1917

IT'S HARD TO FATHOM FROM THE ENDLESS MINING OF JANE AUSTEN'S legacy that this beloved author's reputation, modest enough during her lifetime, began to decline right after it. From the continued quest for Mr. Darcy (think Mark Darcy in *Bridget Jones's Diary*) to the appropriation of Austen's iconic narratives (*Sense and Sensibility and Sea Monsters*) to sequels (*Mr. Darcy Takes a Wife*), to using the books themselves as a device for telling a modern tale of love and friendship (*The Jane Austen Book Club*), there seems to be no such thing as Too Much Jane. And that's without considering all the film and television adaptations of her novels.

It took a posthumous biography by her nephew, James Edward Austen-Leigh, to revive her flagging reputation. Published some fifty years after his aunt's death, it's respectfully written and thorough. Still, it planted some persistent myths about Jane Austen's writing life, such as: "I do not think that she herself was much mortified by the want of early success," he wrote. "She wrote for her own amusement. Money, though acceptable, was not necessary for the moderate expenses of her quiet home."

Austen-Leigh was also the first to set out the idea that Austen was somehow ashamed of her literary endeavors: "She was careful that her occupation should not be suspected by servants, or visitors, or any persons beyond her own family party. She wrote upon small sheets of paper which could easily be put away, or covered with a piece of blotting paper. There was, between the front door and the offices, a swing door which creaked when it was opened; but she objected to having this little inconvenience remedied, because it gave her notice when anyone was coming."

It's difficult to know how accurate these observations were, as Austen-Leigh relied on the memory of scenes occurring decades past, when he was a child. Still, the story gained enough traction that it was perpetuated by Virginia Woolf in *A Room of One's Own*: "At any rate, one would not have been ashamed to have been caught in the act of writing *Pride and Prejudice*. Yet Jane Austen was glad that a hinge creaked, so that she might hide her manuscript before anyone came in. To Jane Austen there was something discreditable in writing *Pride and Prejudice*."

Jane Austen's scant remaining letters tell a different story. She didn't write merely for her own amusement, but was deeply invested in having her work published and read. An avid reader herself, she took for role models several widely published female authors of her time, notably, the critically admired Fanny Burney. Her talent was valued and taken seriously by her entire family; her father, and later her brothers, acted as her agents, working diligently to get her books in print and to preserve her literary reputation. One observation by Austen-Leigh that holds up is that Austen did experience "want of early success." But with persistence and continued effort, interest in her books climbed slowly and steadily. Below you'll see the text from a letter written by her father to a perspective publisher. The letter (written around 1797) likely refers to *Pride and Prejudice*. The publisher didn't even bother to respond to it, and simply sent the original letter back to George Austen by return post. Getting one's original query letter back with a submission makes it quite likely that neither the letter nor the submission received the least bit of attention. If Jane Austen's work suffered such a bruising dismissal, it can happen to anyone; what's left to do is just what the Austens did — repackage the submission, send it out again, and repeat as needed.

Sir — I have in my possession a manuscript novel, comprising 3 vols., about the length of Miss Burney's "Evalina." As I am well aware of what consequence it is that a work of this sort should make its first appearance under a respectable name, I apply to you. I shall be much obliged therefore if you will inform me whether you choose to be concerned in it, what will be the expense of publishing it at the author's risk, and what you will venture to advance for the property of it, if on perusal it is approved of. Should you give any encouragement, I will send you the work.

I am, Sir, your humble Servant,
George Austen

We had very early cherished the dream of one day becoming authors. This dream, never relinquished even when distance divided and absorbing tasks occupied us, now suddenly acquired strength and consistency: it took the character of a resolve. We agreed to arrange a small section of our poems, and, if possible, get them printed. Averse to personal publicity, we veiled our own names under those of Currer, Ellis, and Acton Bell; the ambiguous choice being dictated by a sort of conscientious scruple at assuming Christian names positively masculine, while we did not like to declare ourselves women, because — without at the time suspecting that our mode of writing and thinking was not what is called "feminine" — we had a vague impression that authoresses are liable to be looked on with prejudice...

The book was printed: it is scarcely known, was published and advertised at the sisters' own expense and sold two copies) and all of it that merits to be known are the poems of Ellis Bell...Ill-success failed to crush us: the mere effort to succeed had given a wonderful zest to existence; it must be pursued. We each set to work on a prose tale: Ellis Bell produced *Wuthering Heights,* Acton Bell, *Agnes Grey,* and Currer Bell also wrote a narrative in one volume*. These [manuscripts] were perseveringly obtruded upon various publishers for the space of a year and a half; usually, their fate was an ignominious and abrupt dismissal...

— *Biographical Notice of Ellis and Acton Bell,* 1850
*referring to *The Professor*

MOST RATIONAL WRITERS WOULD AGREE THAT it's impossible for publishers to craft personalized rejection letters to each and every applicant (or should I say, supplicant?) for publication. Yet, form rejection letters are nothing new and universally loathed by writers in all stages of their careers. Charlotte Brontë was as aggrieved as anyone might be by impersonal rejections, or worse yet, lack of any response. Before attempting to publish novels, Charlotte, who seemed to be the front person for the trio of Brontë sisters (consisting of herself, Emily, and Anne), undertook the task of finding a home for a collaborative book of poems under their assumed *noms de plume.* "The book," referred to in the second paragraph at right was dryly titled *Currer, Ellis, and Acton Bell's Poems,* finally did find a home and was published in 1846 to absolutely no fanfare and humiliating sales of two copies.

Bruised but undaunted, Brontë's repeated, unsuccessful efforts to secure a publisher for her first novel were described by her biographer, Elizabeth Gaskell: "*The Professor* had met with many refusals from different publishers, some, I have reason to believe, not over-courteously worded in writing to an unknown author, and none alleging any distinct reason for its rejection is, perhaps, hardly to be expected that, in the press of business in a great publishing house, they should find time to explain why they decline particular works ... I can well sympathise with the published account which 'Currer Bell' gives, of the feelings experienced on reading Messers Smith, Elder & Co.'s letter containing the rejection of *The Professor.*"

This rejection, amplified on the following page, at least offered at least some hope to the disheartened Brontë. The publisher recognized enough incipient talent to encourage the author to submit her next work to them, a practice that's not uncommon even in today's publishing world. Her description of this letter is revealed on the following page.

Charlotte Brontë: Seeing a ray of hope

 Currer Bell's book found acceptance nowhere, nor any acknowledgment of merit, so that something like the chill of despair began to invade his heart. As a forlorn hope, he tried one publishing house more — Messrs Smith and Elder. Ere long, in a much shorter space than that on which experience had taught him to calculate — there came a letter, which he opened in the dreary expectation of finding two hard hopeless lines, intimating that Messrs Smith and Elder "were not disposed to publish the [manuscript]," and, instead, he took out of the envelope a letter of two pages. He read it trembling. It declined, indeed, to publish the tale, for business reasons, but it discussed its merits and demerits so courteously, so considerately, in a spirit so rational, with a discrimination so enlightened, that this very refusal cheered the author better than a vulgarly-expressed acceptance would have done. It was added, that a work in three volumes would meet with careful attention.

— *Biographical Notice of Ellis and Acton Bell*, 1850

... And at last, acceptance

 My work (a tale in one volume) being completed, I offered it to a publisher. He said it was original, faithful to nature, but he did not feel warranted in accepting it; such a work would not sell. I tried six publishers in succession; they all told me it was deficient in "startling incident" and "thrilling excitement," that it would never suit the circulating libraries, and as it was on those libraries the success of works of fiction mainly depended, they could not undertake to publish what would be overlooked there.

  "Jane Eyre" was rather objected to at first, on the same grounds, but finally found acceptance.

— From a letter to G.H. Lewes, 1847

SUBMITTED UNDER HER PEN NAME, CHARLOTTE BRONTË'S "FORLORN" manuscript for *The Professor* was making its rounds and being rejected by half a dozen London publishers. With nowhere near the number of publishing houses as there are today, each disappointment was significant. Adding to the pain was that her sisters' novels (Emily's *Wuthering Heights* and Anne's *Agnes Grey*) found homes, even as hers didn't. Yet Brontë did what any sensible aspiring author would. Instead of sitting by idly, she worked on her next novel.

At last, finally getting some encouragement from Messers Smith and Elder that her next submission might get some careful attention, her next manuscript was at the ready, and she dispatched it, post haste. That new manuscript was none other than *Jane Eyre*. The publisher must have sensed a winner; the book was hastily brought out just six weeks after acceptance, and became an immediate bestseller. *The Professor*, meanwhile, continued to languish, and was published posthumously, remaining one of Brontë's more obscure works.

If you've ever had a manuscript that was continually ignored or rejected by publishers, those evaluating it (or ignoring it) may have been right or wrong about its merits, or lack thereof. But Charlotte Brontë's strategy was spot-on. Rather than pining away for news while a work is making its rounds, there's no better remedy for anxious anticipation than to delve into a new project.

I now send you per rail a MS entitled Jane Eyre, a novel in three volumes, by Currer Bell. I find I cannot prepay the carriage of the parcel, as money for that purpose is not received at the small station-house where it is left. If, when you acknowledge the receipt of the MS, you would have the goodness to mention the amount charged on delivery, I will immediately transmit it in postage stamps. It is better in future to address Mr Currer Bell, under cover to Miss Brontë, Haworth, Bradford, Yorkshire, as there is a risk of letters otherwise directed not reaching me at present ...

— Charlotte Brontë, from a letter to a prospective publisher, 1847

L.M. MONTGOMERY:
REJECTION CAN BE A BLESSING IN DISGUISE

 Today I read an article in which the writer spoke of a book he had once hoped to write and never would. This set me thinking of the book I planned to write — but never did. There were several of them in my early teens, all carefully "thought out" and quite complete in my mental storehouse. Many a night I lay awake in that old farmhouse by the eastern sea — many an evening I walked alone in the afterglow of autumnal sunsets — composing them and a jolly good time I had of it.

I did write a book whereof no record remaineth. It was back I think in '99 or '00. I intended it for a "Sunday School Library Book" — thinking that if I could get it accepted by one of the religious publishing houses I might make a few hundreds out of it…I thought then — and still think — that it was every whit as good as nine out of ten of the Sunday School stories that found publishers. I sent it away to the Presbyterian Board of Publications in Philadelphia and when they refused it I sent it to the Congregational Publishing Society of Boston. Back it came. I never sent it out again.

 Probably if I had kept on I might have found a publisher. I am exceedingly thankful I did not. To have had that book accepted would have been the greatest misfortune that ever happened to "my literary career." I could never have risen above it; and it would probably have committed me to a lifetime of writing "series" similar to it.

But I did not realize my lucky escape at the time. The cloud of disappointment seemed to have no silver lining and I cried myself to sleep for a week over the downfall of my humble little castle of dreams.

— From her journal, entry dated July 1925

MARJORIE KINNAN RAWLINGS (1896–1953), THE mid-twentieth century author best known for her Pulitzer Prize-winning young adult novel *The Yearling,* honed her craft as a newspaper reporter. And like other authors who started out this way (including Willa Cather, Edna Ferber, and L.M. Montgomery), she longed to take her writing in a more artistic direction. Starting with the short story form, she wrote to what she thought were market dictates, to no avail:

"I tried to write what I thought they [the popular magazines] would be most likely to buy and all that brought me was rejection slips. Then in 1928 I had an opportunity to buy an orange grove in Florida and I bought it, left the newspaper and settled down to give all my time to fiction. Still the stories didn't sell so I gave up. I thought the best thing might be to write poetry — that would satisfy the urge to create and would bother no one ... But then I thought — just one more. And I wrote a story that seemed far from 'commercial,' that — it seemed to me — no editor would want to buy but that had meaning for me. It sold like a shot and I've had no trouble selling since, though I never have tried to write 'commercially.'"

Early on, L.M. Montgomery also tried writing to suit a market. That the rejection came from an arena to which she was ill-suited did nothing to assuage her bitter tears, but with perspective she realized that falling into the wrong niche would have brought nothing but regret. Writing to sell to specific markets is something that writers do — and have done — as a way to make a living, and there's nothing wrong with that. But affecting a style that plainly isn't "you," or pursuing a subject you care nothing about as a way to get a foot in the door — those are slippery slopes that are hard to climb back from. To be rejected for *not* being yourself, as Montgomery and Rawlings have demonstrated, can be a valuable gift to a writer, especially one just coming into her own.

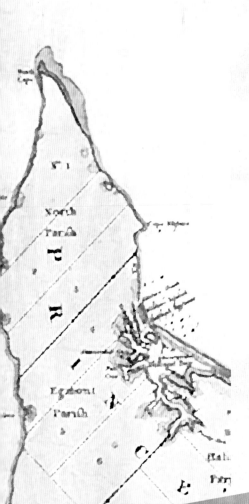

LIKE MANY AUTHORS BATTERED BY CONTINUAL rejection of a manuscript, L.M. Montgomery gave up. She placed the worn *Anne of Green Gables* manuscript in a hatbox. After it languished in a freezing attic for nearly a year, Maud, as she was known to her familiars, decided to give it one more shot, sending it to Boston publisher L.C. Page. Serendipitously, there she had an ally — a Prince Edward Island expatriate named Miss Arbuckle. One of the company's readers, she was enchanted with the novel's romanticized Island setting. Miss Arbuckle "quietly and persistently championed Anne to the other staff readers until several supported the novel," according to Mary Rubio and Elizabeth Waterston in *Writing a Life*. *Anne of Green Gables* promptly became a bestseller, and has brought joy to readers for generations since.

I know many writers who have toiled for years on a project (myself included), only to set it aside for the flimsiest of reasons. The manuscript gets shoved into our own versions of Montgomery's attic — usually a drawer or closet, perhaps never to see the light of day again. When a rudimentary version of this book started feeling too complicated, I put it away in a box. A trip to The Mount (Edith Wharton's one-time home) reignited my interest in it, and you're holding the result in your hands. What if Maud Montgomery hadn't decided to dust off the manuscript and give her dream one more shot at success? You may have a manuscript or idea you can revisit and improve. There's nothing sweeter than realizing a dream deferred.

L.M. MONTGOMERY: ONE MORE TRY

I have always kept a notebook in which I jotted down, as they occurred to me, ideas for plots, incidents, characters and descriptions. Two years ago in the spring of 1905 I was looking over this notebook in search of some suitable idea for a short serial I wanted to write for a certain Sunday School paper and I found a faded entry, written ten years before: — "Elderly couple apply to orphan asylum for a boy. By mistake a girl is sent them." I thought this would do. I began to block out chapters, devise incidents and "brood up" my heroine. Somehow or other she seemed very real to me and I thought it rather a shame to waste her on an ephemeral little serial. Then the thought came, "Write a book about her. You have the central idea and character. All you have to do is spread it out over enough chapters to amount to a book."

The result of this was "Anne of Green Gables." I began the actual writing of it one evening in May and wrote most of it in the evenings after my regular work was done, through that summer and autumn, finishing it, I think, sometime in January 1906. It was a labor of love. Nothing I have written gave me so much pleasure to write. I cast "moral" and "Sunday School" ideals to the winds and made my Anne a real human girl. Many of my own childhood experiences and dreams were worked up into its chapters...I typewrote it out on my old second-hand typewriter that never makes the capitals plain and doesn't print "w" at all. The next thing was to find a publisher. I sent it to the Bobbs-Merrill firm of Indianapolis...This was a new firm that had recently come to the front with several " bestsellers." I thought I might stand a better chance with a new firm than with an old established one which

Continued on the next page

had already a preferred list of writers. Bobbs-Merrill very promptly sent it back with a formal printed slip of rejection. I had a cry of disappointment. Then I went to the other extreme and sent it to the MacMillan Co. of New York, arguing that perhaps an "old established firm" might be more inclined to take a chance with a new writer. The MacMillan Co. likewise sent it back. I did not cry this time but sent it to Lothrop, Lee and Shepard of Boston, a sort of "betwixt and between" firm. They sent it back. Then I sent it to Henry Holt and Co. of New York. They rejected it, but not with the formal printed slip of the others. They sent a typewritten screed stating that their readers had found "some merit" in the story but "not enough to warrant its acceptance." This "damning with faint praise" flattened me out as not even the printed slips could do. I put "Anne" away in an old hat box in the clothes room, resolving that some day when I had time I would cut her down to the seven chapters of my original idea and send her to the aforesaid Sunday School paper.

The MS lay in the hat box until one day last winter when I came across it during a rummage. I began turning over the sheets, reading a page here and there. Somehow, I found it rather interesting. Why shouldn't other people find it so? "I'll try once more" I said and I sent it to the L.C. Page Co. They

We take pleasure in advising you that our readers report favorably with regard to your girls' story "Anne of Green Gables," and if mutually satisfactory arrangements can be made, we shall be glad to add the book to our next season's list.

took it and asked me to write a sequel to it. The book may or may not sell well. I wrote it for love, not money — but very often such books are the most successful — just as everything in life that is born of true love is better than something constructed for mercenary ends.

I don't know what kind of publisher I've got. I know absolutely nothing of the Page Co. They have given me a royalty of ten percent of the wholesale price, which is not generous even for a new writer, and they have bound me to give them all my books on the same terms for five years. I didn't altogether like this but I was afraid to protest, lest they might not take the book, and I am so anxious to get it before the public. It will be a start, even if it is no great success. Well, I've written my book. The dream dreamed years ago in that old brown desk in school has come true after years of toil and struggle. And the realization is sweet — almost as sweet as the dream!

— From her journal, entry dated August 1907

To-day has been, as Anne herself would say, 'an epoch in my life.' My book came to-day ... from the publishers. I candidly confess that it was to me a proud and wonderful and thrilling moment. There, in my hand, lay the material realization of all the dreams and hopes and ambitions and struggles of my whole conscious existence — my first book. Not a great book, but mine, mine, mine, something which I have created.

— L.M. Montgomery
  The Alpine Path, 1917

THERE'S NO BETTER STORY TO ILLUSTRATE THE fine line between rejection and acceptance than the one told by Madeleine L'Engle: "*A Wrinkle in Time* was almost never published," she wrote. "You can't name a major publisher who didn't reject it. When we'd run through forty-odd publishers, my agent sent it back. We gave up." Most editors thought it too dark for children.

After some time, L'Engle made contact with John Farrar of Farrar Straus Giroux through a friend of her mother's, and the rest is publishing history. Published in 1962, *A Wrinkle in Time* has the distinction of having won some of the most prestigious publishing awards, including the prestigious Newbery. It's still in print, with millions of copies sold, and interestingly, is also one of the most frequently banned books of all time. Despite the fact that L'Engle was a devout Christian, its detractors objected to the book's themes on religious grounds.

Did L'Engle's books help make complex children's literature more palatable to publishers? Evidently, children have long proven themselves ready for books like *A Wrinkle in Time* (which, to put it simply, tells a tale of the triumph of love, loyalty, and creativity over conformity, brainwashing, and evil). This is borne out most abundantly by the unparalleled success of the *Harry Potter* series. Much has been made of the initial rejections of the first installment of J.K. Rowling's blockbuster series, but hers were the more usual numbers of rejections before an agent and publisher recognized the talent and potential of this then-unknown writer. Her path wasn't smooth, to be sure, but it may have been much rougher had it not been for authors like Madeleine L'Engle who came before her.

When my book was rejected by publisher after publisher, I cried out in my journal. I wrote, after an early rejection, "X turned down *Wrinkle,* turned it down with one hand while saying that he loved it, but didn't quite dare do it, as it isn't really classifiable, and am wondering if I'll have to go through the usual hell with this that I seem to go through with everything that I write. But this book I'm sure of...And yesterday morning before we left, there was a letter from Hugh saying that X has turned down *Wrinkle.* Perhaps I'm becoming slowly inured. I went through a few hours of the usual primitive despairing rage, but I could show none of it as I was with the children driving down to the city. Am I really getting so that I can stand it better? Perhaps the fury and bitterness builds up.

...In a book I'm reading about Fitzgerald, there is a sentence about "second-rate writers who pass themselves off as geniuses." But how does anybody know? A writer is far too tied up in his work, if [she] is really a writer, to know whether it is second-rate or a work of genius. And how many writers who have been considered second-rate, and yet have persisted in believing in themselves, have been discovered and hailed as geniuses after their deaths / or writers who have been highly acclaimed during their lives have been forgotten forever shortly after? Or writers who are true geniuses have never been discovered at all? ... I for once have the arrogance to know in my heart that this is something good. But if it is constantly turned down will I be able to keep the faith that I still have in it? Will I begin to doubt?"

— *A Circle of Quiet,* 1972

Madeleine L'Engle:
"Like the rejection of me, myself"

 Well, somehow or other, like a lot of other women who have quite deliberately and happily chosen to be mothers, and work at another vocation as well, I did manage to get a lot of writing done. But during that decade when I was in my thirties, I couldn't sell anything. If a writer says [she] doesn't care whether [she] is published or not, I don't believe [her]. I care. Undoubtedly I care too much. But we do not write for ourselves alone. I write about what concerns me, and I want to share my concerns. I want what I write to be read. Every rejection slip — and you could paper walls with my rejection slips — was like the rejection of me, myself, and certainly of my *amour-propre.* I learned all kinds of essential lessons during those years of rejection, and I'm glad to have had them, but I wouldn't want to have to go through them again ... I was, perhaps, out of joint with time.

Two of my books for children were rejected for reasons which would be considered absurd today. Publisher after publisher turned down *Meet the Austins* because it begins with a death. Publisher after publisher turned down *A Wrinkle in Time* because it deals overtly with the problem of evil, and it was too difficult for children, and was it a children's or an adults' book, anyhow?

... I didn't dread being forty; I looked forward to it. My thirties had been such a rough decade in so many ways that I was eager for change. Surely, with the new decade, luck would turn. On my birthday I was, as usual, out in the Tower working on a book. The children were in school. My husband was at work and would be getting the mail. He called, saying, "I'm sorry to have to tell you this on your birthday, but you'd never trust me again if I kept it from you. They have rejected *The Lost Innocent.*"

This seemed an obvious sign from heaven. I should stop trying to write. All during the decade of my thirties (the world's fifties) I went through spasms of guilt because I spent so much time writing, because I wasn't like a good New England housewife and mother. When I scrubbed the kitchen floor, the family cheered. I couldn't make decent pie crust. I always managed to get something red in with the white laundry in the washing machine, so that everybody wore streaky pink underwear. And with all the hours I spent writing, I was still not pulling my own weight financially.

So the rejection on the fortieth birthday seemed an unmistakable command: Stop this foolishness and learn to make cherry pie.

I covered the typewriter in a great gesture of renunciation. Then I walked around and around the room, bawling my head off. I was totally, unutterably miserable. Suddenly I stopped, because I realized what my subconscious mind was doing while I was sobbing: my subconscious mind was busy working out a novel about failure.

I uncovered the typewriter. In my journal I recorded this moment of decision, for that's what it was. I had to write. I had no choice in the matter. It was not up to me to say I would stop, because I could not. It didn't matter how small or inadequate my talent. If I never had another book published, I still had to go on writing.

I'm glad I made this decision in the moment of failure. It's easy to say you're a writer when things are going well. When the decision is made in the abyss, then it is quite clear that it is not one's decision at all.

— *A Circle of Quiet,* 1972

Louisa May Alcott: To begin "Little Women"

 May, 1868 — Mr. N. wants a girls' story, and I begin "Little Women." Marmee, Anna, and May all approve my plan. So I plod away, though I don't enjoy this sort of thing. Never liked girls or knew many, except my sisters; but our queer plays and experiences may prove interesting, though I doubt it.

June. — Sent twelve chapters of "L.W." to Mr. N. He thought it *dull,* and so do I. But work away and mean to try the experiment; for lively, simple books are very much needed for girls, and perhaps I can supply the need.

August. — Roberts Bros. made an offer for the story, but at the same time advised me to keep the copyright; so I shall.

— From her journal
Entries dated May–August 1868

"It reads better than I expected"

 August, 26, 1868 — Proof of whole book came. It reads better than I expected. Not a bit sensational, but simple and true, for we really lived most of it; and if it succeeds that will be the reason of it. Mr. N. likes it better now and says some girls who have read the manuscript say it is "splendid"! As it is for them, they are the best critics, so I should be satisfied.

October 30. — First edition gone and more called for. Expects to sell three or four thousand before the new year.

Mr. N. wants a second volume for spring. Pleasant notices and letters arrive, and much interest in my little women, who seem to find friends by their truth to life, as I hoped.

— From her journal
Entries dated August–October 1868

The first serious novel Louisa May Alcott published under her real name was *Moods*. Released in 1864 following many pseudonymous thrillers and gothics, *Moods* built on the moderate yet solid success of *Hospital Sketches*, nonfiction pieces about her experiences as a Civil War nurse. Critical and public reception of her first attempt at literary fiction was disappointing and left its author dejected. Weary of churning out the sensational tales that were her financial mainstay, Alcott's literary identity was adrift from the time of *Moods'* publication until 1868, when she penned the book that would change her life.

Taking up her publisher's request to try a "girls' story," she cranked out *Little Women* in two and a half months, though her heart wasn't in it. Neither she nor her publisher thought highly of the results. Amazingly, the entire proof of the book was produced in the same month that the publisher made an offer for it; the young readers of the proof loved it (think of them as an early version of a focus group) and advance orders were quite pleasing. *Little Women* was an immediate bestseller, exceeding expectations of both the author and publisher. It has been passed on by women of each generation since to their daughters, nieces, and younger friends as a must-read classic with universal themes. With typical self-deprecation, Alcott describes how readily she sold work to publishers after becoming a bestselling author: "Funny time with the publishers about the tale; for all wanted it at once, and each tried to outbid the other for an unwritten story," she wrote in an 1874 journal entry. "I rather enjoyed it, and felt important with Roberts, Low, and Scribner all clamoring for my ''umble' works. No more peddling poor little manuscripts now, and feeling rich with $10."

Self-acceptance came after the "simple and true" novel that emerged from the pen of its reluctant author was embraced by an enthusiastic audience. Alcott had experimented with a number of styles to see which might bring her some measure of success. Most everyone who writes does this to a greater or lesser extent — it's like trying on different outfits to see which is most suitable. Sometimes, what turns out to be really "you" isn't what fits your own preconceived notions. *Little Women* may not have been the kind of book Alcott preferred for bringing her fame. But she was satisfied that the work's honest style had finally brought her the renown and financial security she had so long desired.

FROM HER DISAPPROVING MOTHER, TO HER ERSTWHILE HUSBAND, to her snooty society friends, Edith Wharton lived in a milieu that reinforced her deep insecurity and sense of non-belonging. Her first tentative steps into the literary world, the place she most longed to be, met with a steady acceptance from the critics and public that took her by surprise. It took many small victories — published stories, books, and warm reviews — before Wharton believed she was worthy of any such success. "The doing of *The Decoration of Houses* amused me very much, but can hardly be regarded as part of my literary career," she wrote of her first published book (on the subject of interior design, co-authored with a colleague).

Her "real career," as she called it, started with the sale of a few short stories to *Scribner's Magazine*, which in turn, led to the publication of her first collection of stories (*The Greater Inclination*) in 1899. With mingled incredulity and pleasure, she described the accepted work as "stories which editors wanted for their magazines, and a publisher actually wanted for a volume!" She vowed to turn away from the "distractions of a busy and sociable life, full of friends and travel and gardening for the discipline of the daily task." As she wrote in her memoir, this is when she went from being "a drifting amateur to a professional," and, most importantly, "gained what I lacked most — self-confidence."

Wharton's steadily climbing career was punctuated with major honors, including the Pulitzer Prize for the Novel (as it was then called) for *The Age of Innocence*, awarded to her in 1921. She was the first woman to achieve this distinction. Two years later she also became the first woman ever to receive an honorary doctorate (conferred by Yale University). Edith Wharton finally reconciled public acceptance of her as an accomplished author with her own self-image.

Not long ago, I was browsing in the home renovation and decor section of a bookstore for a gift for someone who had recently bought a historic house to refurbish. Among all the contemporary books, I was delighted to see a copy of Edith Wharton's *The Decoration of Houses* (originally published in 1897) in a recently reissued edition. I imagined how amazed she would be that the book she disparaged was still in print after more than a hundred years. Then, I thought of my own long foray as a cookbook author. Though I'm hardly willing to discard this part of my career out of hand, as Wharton did with her domestic nonfiction titles, I welcome a continued learning curve ahead in which a different kind of body of work can emerge — honorary doctorates optional.

I had written short stories that were thought worthy of preservation! Was it the same insignificant *I* that I had always known? Any one walking along the streets might go into any bookshop, and say "Please give me Edith Wharton's book," and the clerk, without bursting into incredulous laughter, would produce it, and be paid for it, and the purchaser would walk home with it and read it, and talk of it, and pass it on to other people to read! The whole business seemed too unreal to be anything but a practical joke played on me by some occult humourist; and my friends could not have been more astonished and incredulous than I was. I opened the first notices of the book with trembling hands and a suffocated heart. What I had done was actually thought important enough to be not only printed but reviewed! With a sense of mingled guilt and self-satisfaction I glanced at one article after another. They were unbelievably kind, but for the most part their praise only humbled me; and often I found it bewildering.

— *A Backward Glance,* 1934

My long experimenting had resulted in two or three books which brought me more encouragement than I had ever dreamed of obtaining, and were the means of my making some of the happiest friendships of my life. The reception of my books gave me the self-confidence I had so long lacked, and in the company of people who shared my tastes, and treated me as their equal, I ceased to suffer from the agonizing shyness which used to rob such encounters of all pleasure.

— Edith Wharton,
A Backward Glance, 1934

VIRGINIA WOOLF'S NEED FOR APPROVAL WAS VAST, and she sought it from her husband, friends, publishers, and critics. Still, though she cared deeply about the opinions of others, she had the bravery to create works that were experimental and far ahead of their time. *Jacob's Room* (her third novel), for example, which moves into the realm of inner consciousness that became one of the hallmarks of her work, unfolds in a nonlinear fashion. In the quotation at right, she basks in the acceptance letter and praise of her American publisher — the first wholly impartial appraisal she considered herself to have received.

The acceptance of a piece of writing for publication, whether it's your first endeavor or your twentieth, then its subsequent embrace (one hopes!) by the reading public and media are affirming experiences. In many cases, this kind of acknowledgment that your work is print-worthy precede self-acceptance. Looking at the trajectories of the Literary Ladies, it seems that some sort of outside validation was a necessary component of self-acceptance, adding up to the totality of one's identity as an author. Yet self-realization, even among such talented women, was more often than not a hard-won battle.

There's a little cartoon that charmingly illuminates women's struggle with identity. Two caterpillars are creeping along, with a butterfly floating above. One caterpillar eyes the butterfly with suspicion and says, "You'll never catch me going up in one of those things!" A few years ago, in a fit of frustration, I lamented to my journal, "I wish I were a snake who could shed its skin! I'd just slither out and become a butterfly." Mixed metaphor aside, so many of us are like that caterpillar, who's going to become a butterfly despite its qualms. We will also take flight after much toil, trial and error, and rejection. Sometimes acceptance of the new version of ourselves lags behind what others have already perceived about us: we're already aloft, like that butterfly; we just need the courage to lose sight of the ground below.

I am a little uppish ... and self-assertive, because Brace wrote to me yesterday, "We think 'Jacob's Room' an extraordinarily distinguished and beautiful work. You have, of course, your own method, and it is not easy to foretell how many readers it will have; surely it will have enthusiastic ones, and we delight in publishing it ... " As this is my first testimony from an impartial person I am pleased. For one thing it must make some impression, as a whole; and cannot be wholly frigid fireworks.

— *A Writer's Diary*, entry dated October 4, 1922

*W*on't teach any more if I can help it; don't like it; and if I can get writing enough can do much better. I have done more than I had hoped. Supported myself, helped May, and sent something home. Not borrowed a penny, and had only five dollars given me.

— Louisa May Alcott
  From her journal,
  entry dated April 1859

MANY WRITERS DREAM OF BEING ABLE TO MAKE A LIVING AT WHAT THEY love. But loving to write and making money at it don't often go hand in hand, nor must they. If earning money at writing is truly your intent (or if you've achieved this), more power to you. In that event, you'll enjoy basking in the reflected glory of our esteemed authors, all of whom at some point in their careers made a living by the pen, some modestly, and others quite handsomely. This chapter takes a look at the role money played in the writing lives of several of the Literary Ladies; as is true for people in general, some enjoyed talk about finances, while others were silent on the subject.

Making a living at any creative field requires a good deal of calculation and often some compromise. If one is determined to profit from writing, there are many ways to do so aside from pursuing the elusive dream of penning a masterwork of modern literature and hoping it finds a place on the bestseller list. Niche markets for nonfiction will always exist; books and magazines on writers' markets and web sites like WOW! Women on Writing (wow-womenonwriting.com) give solid advice to this end; and, competitive though they may be, teaching gigs and grants help augment writing incomes as well.

The Literary Ladies spanned the gamut, from keeping their writing practice separate from money-making almost entirely (as Anaïs Nin did, though only up to a certain point in her life) to trying to make every word billable (like Louisa May Alcott did, from her first small payments to her later substantial income). Many of the Literary Ladies *had* to work, and chose to make writing their paid vocation because their talent made it possible (and profitable) to do so. Those who achieved success treasured their financial independence, especially in bygone times when this kind of freedom was rare for women. On the flip side is the completely viable choice of writing without giving a second thought to financial outcome, purely for one's own enjoyment or for recording a life in progress. Sitting down to work with compensation foremost on your mind can be a real creativity-killer until and unless you've gotten used to writing to meet actual deadlines. Creative effort can't always be tabulated in dollars and cents.

The passage at right tidily sums up how money and writing can coexist peacefully and practically — never an easy feat. Alcott valued her skills, planned her time conscientiously, and always put something away for the future. The making of "merry" for comfort and pleasure that she found so reassuring would be a well-deserved reward for any of us who write for compensation, or aspire to do so.

Louisa May Alcott:
Small payments do add up

 Things look promising for the new year … $20 for the little tales, and wrote two every month. $25 for the "Bells;" $100 for the two "Proverb" stories. L. takes all I'll send; and F. seems satisfied.

So my plan will work well, and I shall make my $1,000 this year in spite of sickness and worry. Praise the Lord and keep busy, say I.

I am pretty well, and keep so busy I haven't time to be sick … I often think as I go larking round, independent, with more work that I can do, and half-a-dozen publishers asking for tales, of the old times when I went meekly from door to door peddling my first poor little stories, and feeling so rich for $10.

… Keep all the money I send; pay up every bill; get comforts and enjoy yourselves. Let's be merry while we may, and lay up a bit for a rainy day.

— From a letter to her mother, 1868

*P*eople usually ask, "How much have you made?" I am contented with a hundred thousand, & find my best success in the comfort my family enjoy; also a naughty satisfaction in proving that it was better not to "stick to teaching" as advised, but to write.

— Louisa May Alcott
From a letter to journalist Frank Carpenter, 1887

"OVER A HUNDRED LETTERS FROM BOYS & GIRLS, & many from teachers & parents assure me that my little books are read & valued in a way I never dreamed of seeing them. This success is more agreeable to me than money or reputation," Louisa May Alcott commented in 1872. Anything close to the $100,000 figure Alcott quotes at left was a fortune in her day. However modestly Alcott viewed her talent, she didn't shy away from demanding what she felt her work was worth, even before she became a bestselling author.

Alcott made monetary compensation a priority in a way that many writers — male or female — still don't. Because creative work is often so poorly paid, it's accepted that it should be done for love rather than money. Likely, this is a healthy acceptance of a reality. But another reality is that many writers *would* like to be paid for what they do — fairly, if not handsomely. There is a notable lack of cultural support for the creative arts in the U.S., leaving each artist and writer to fashion his or her own solution to the problem of finding the time and means to create, as well as support oneself.

A recent study by the National Endowment for the Arts found that the median income for published female authors is still 70 to 80 percent of that of male authors. I can't help but imagine that the more money-savvy Literary Ladies would wonder at this. In her memoir *Long Quiet Highway,* writing mentor Natalie Goldberg asserts: "Success is none of our business. It comes from the outside. Our job is to write, not look up from our notebook and wonder how much money Norman Mailer earns." This attitude might serve many writers well, but would Louisa May Alcott have agreed? She made success very much her business and insisted on her right to compensation. Though it may not be for everyone, those who truly want to make a living at writing need to look up, ask and expect, and not live on hope that it will somehow happen if it's meant to be.

When I had the youth I had no money; now I have the money I have no time; and when I get the time, if I ever do, I shall have no health to enjoy life. I suppose it's the discipline I need; but it's rather hard to love the things I do and see them go by because duty chains me to my galley .

— Louisa May Alcott
From her journal,
entry dated January 1874

People are more ready to borrow and praise, than to buy — which I cannot wonder at: but tho' I like praise as well as anybody, I like what Edward calls Pewter too.

— Jane Austen
From a letter to a friend
(Fanny Knight), 1814

PICTURE JANE AUSTEN IN HER COUNTRY HOME, wearing her frilly cap, quill in hand. She writes because the fires of genius compel her to, and she doesn't give two cents about twopence, or any other denomination of financial remuneration. She's too genteel for that. Wrong! Austen was keenly interested in business affairs that pertained to her literary endeavors.

Jane Austen wasn't "discovered" in any major way; she and her family opted for some of the venues for publishing available to them, none all that attractive or profitable. Unable to find a good home for *Pride and Prejudice,* they embarked on a similar mission for *Sense and Sensibility.* At last, they found a reputable publisher, Thomas Egerton, to print it on a commission basis. She was eager to see it in print, regardless of the method, and wrote to her sister, "I am never too busy to think of *Sense and Sensibility.* I can no more forget it, than a mother can forget her suckling child." It was published in 1811 and took two years to sell out the edition of one thousand. When another printing was ordered, she wrote to Cassandra, "I cannot help hoping that *many* will feel themselves obliged to buy it."

Pride and Prejudice was soon after also taken by Egerton with little fanfare and even less favorable terms. The Austens decided to sell the copyright outright, as that was another route to getting published. She received £110, and wrote in a letter, "I would rather have had £150, but we could not both be pleased, & I am not at all surprised that he should not chuse [sic] to hazard so much." The book was published to critical acclaim in 1813, and was one of the most successful novels of the season. Its author identified on the title page only as "A Lady." The publisher went through three printings in her lifetime, but having sold the copyright (which lasted twenty-eight years), she received no further remuneration.

Despite modest sales by today's standards, *Pride and Prejudice* and *Sense and Sensibility* were deemed successes, and set the stage for slow and steady sales of her subsequent books.

Austen eagerly awaited payments, and knew just when to expect them, not unlike contemporary authors who hang about the mailbox when royalty time comes along. In total, she earned about £680 for her books in her lifetime, not a dazzling sum, but the receipt of which gave her great pleasure. It's difficult to know just how significant this sum was to the Austens, but to put it in just a bit of perspective, the dowry of her renowned fictional heroine, Elizabeth Bennett, is worth £1,000. Elizabeth's future husband, Mr. Darcy, has an income of £10,000 a year, the equivalent of a millionaire's.

Charlotte Brontë, a generation later, used the name "Currer Bell," not merely a pen name but also a male alter ego to represent herself in business affairs. When *Jane Eyre* became an immediate bestseller and public sensation, she received her first royalty payment of £100. Still under the guise of "Currer Bell," she wrote to her publisher's representative, "I was glad and proud to get the bank bill Mr. Smith sent me yesterday." It was the largest amount of money she'd ever seen, and a far sight more than her annual wage of £20 a year earned as a governess. She was to receive four more such payments for her masterwork; its success set the stage for her next two works, *Shirley* and *Villette*.

Would Jane Austen and Charlotte Brontë, or any of the other Literary Ladies, for that matter, have continued to write without financial reward? I'm confident that most would have, though they may have been less content with doing so than our romantic notions of them might lead us to believe. Perhaps the youthful Sylvia Plath summed up the quandary best: "You do it for itself first. If it brings in money, how nice. You do not do it first for money. Money isn't why you sit down at the typewriter. Not that you don't want it. It is only too lovely when a profession pays for your bread and butter. With writing, it is maybe, maybe-not."

POOR MAUD MONTGOMERY. EVEN A HANDSOME ROYALTY CHECK was no salve for her troubled spirits. In 1910, a royalty check of $7,000 (for her first novel, *Anne of Green Gables*) was an enormous sum of money, and one that came to her at the beginning of her considerable career. At the time she received it, the income for the average worker on Prince Edward Island was just $300 a year! Her journals reveal pride in her accomplishment: "It seems that *Anne* is a big success. It is a 'bestseller' and in its fifth edition ... I can't believe that such a simple little tale, written in and of a simple Prince Edward Island farming settlement, with a juvenile audience in view, can really have scored out in the busy world." Yet such fleeting joy was followed with entries like this: "I have had a month of nervous prostration — an utter breakdown of body, soul, and spirit. The hideous suffering of it, especially of the first fortnight, is something of which the mere remembrance curdles my blood." This was her depression speaking.

Like many a first-time author, Montgomery was so eager to grab that first book deal that she signed her first contract without really understanding it. And, not wanting to rock the boat, she didn't ask questions. Her lack of business acumen proved costly, as it led some years later to a legal suit against Page & Co., her first publisher, for withholding royalties and selling reprint rights without her permission. As part of a settlement, she sold rights to the publisher for what she thought was a generous sum, only to see Page turn around and sell screen and stage rights; Montgomery could do nothing but watch as the popularity of her spirited red-haired orphan soared via various dramatic adaptations, though she received no further compensation for her early works.

If L.M. Montgomery were with us still, she might caution newly minted authors and seasoned ones alike to consult an agent or an attorney, and to understand what they're signing. Despite being burned financially, just three years after the suit she seemed able to put the ordeal behind her, confident in her ability to build on her reputation.

L.M. Montgomery: What good is money now?

I received my publisher's report today and the year's royalty check — over seven thousand dollars! It seems like mockery that this money should come to me now when I am perhaps too broken even to enjoy it. If I could only have had one tenth of that sum when I was a young girl, struggling for an education and enduring many humiliations and disappointments because of my lack of money. A little of it then would have saved me much. Nevertheless, I suppose it is not to be despised even now, if I ever regain health and spirit to enjoy it.

— *From her journal,* entry dated February, 1910

Indeed, money can't buy happiness

Last night I sat down and computed the number of dollars I have made by my pen since that day in Halifax twenty-five years ago when I got my first check — five dollars for a story. The result totals up to about one hundred thousand dollars. Not such a bad total, considering the equipment I started out with — my pen and a knack of expression. If Pages had not been rogues I should have had at least fifty thousand more. But it's not so bad. It's a pity it doesn't mean happiness. But perhaps my children will reap the happiness from it that I cannot have. And perhaps they would be better off, and more ambitious and successful if they had to scramble along and struggle as I did. That seems often to be the way in this mad world.

— *From her journal,* entry dated February, 1921

George Sand: "I like to give money away"

 I don't believe in all the sorrows that people predict for me in the literary career on which I'm trying to embark. You have to know and appreciate what motives drive me and what goal I'm pursuing. My husband has fixed my living allowance at 3,000 francs. You know that's not much for me, for I like to give money away, and not bother counting. I therefore think only of improving my well-being through some earnings, and as I've no desire to be known, I won't be. I will attract neither the envy nor hatred of anyone. Most writers are nourished by bitterness and battles, I know, but those that have no other ambition to make a living, live in the shade, peacefully.

— From a letter to a friend (Jules Boucoiran), 1831

"I live by my day's work"

 I have not a sou in the world. I live by my day's work as does the proletarian; when I can no longer do my day's work, I shall be packed up for the other world, and then I shall have no more need of anything.

...No, I have not what you call worries about money; my revenues are very small, but they are sure...Unless I have extraordinary reverses, I shall have enough to feed me and warm me until the end of my days. My heirs are or will be rich (for it is I who am the poor one of the family...).

As for gaining money by my pen, that is an aspiration that I have never had, recognizing that I was radically incapable of it.

— From a letter to Gustave Flaubert, 1867

IT'S A GOOD THING THAT GEORGE SAND NOT ONLY inherited the lovely Nohant estate described on page 102, but became financially independent early on thanks to her incredible literary output. In the letter at the top of the facing page, she is a young aspiring writer, trapped in a loveless marriage to her first husband. She fled to Paris, leaving her husband temporarily in charge of their two young children. To earn money, she worked as a journalist at the newspaper *Le Figaro*, the first woman ever to do so. However, she denigrated the job, describing it as "the meanest of work," while determined, despite detractors, to launch her literary career. Nevertheless, she found some value in her day job, writing to a friend in 1831, "It affords me the opportunity of making most useful and amusing observations." She returned to collect her children once she had found her financial footing.

Should Sand have been dependent on a man, their major arguments could well have been over her "money style," which was to spend lavishly. The more she made, the more she gave away. Oddly, while obsessively turning out stories, novels, plays, and essays, she claimed that she didn't write for money's sake. Though Sand took pains to seem unconcerned about money, she needed it, wanted it, and relied only on herself to ensure her family's comfort and her own considerable pleasures.

While it's difficult to admit, when it comes to money, I've been, until now, more of a George Sand, spending my earnings blithely (then wondering where it all goes). Learning about Louisa May Alcott and Edna Ferber, who kept scrupulous track of their incomes and knew how every cent was spent, has been a wake-up call. The Literary Ladies who lived to see small fortunes made from their work in their lifetimes savored the benefits: travel, ease from worry, and above all, the ability to take good care of their families. They demonstrated that being practical about money doesn't mean self-denial, and that putting some away for a rainy day is especially critical for women in such uncertain creative professions.

As for me, when money comes, I say, "So much the better," without excitement, and if it does not come, I say, "So much the worse," without any chagrin. Money not being the aim, ought not to be the preoccupation. It is, moreover, not the real proof of success, since so many vapid or poor things make money.

— George Sand
From a letter to Gustave Flaubert, 1868

As we've learned, many of the Literary Ladies worked at ancillary forms of writing to make extra money. Some stopped doing such "day jobs" just as soon as their books began making money; others, for whom financial pressures were ceaseless, continued to take on extra work. Virginia Woolf, for example, wrote criticism and essays while her literary reputation modestly and steadily increased. With her husband, Leonard Woolf, she founded Hogarth Press. It started as a hobby to print fine, limited editions of literary works. The press gradually grew to accommodate some notable authors from their Bloomsbury circle and beyond, and enjoyed some bestseller successes, notably, the novels of Vita Sackville-West. Some of Virginia Woolf's novels were published by the press once it gained prestige — a case of publishing close to the vest, rather than self-publishing. She also acted as editor and sometimes marketer for the press, much to her chagrin.

For all the fame and fortune *Uncle Tom's Cabin* earned Harriet Beecher Stowe in the 1850s, she continued to write articles and sketches while working on subsequent novels. Financial need apparently played a large role. In 1868, she wrote a heartfelt letter to her publisher, James Fields, bemoaning the fact that she was "constantly tempted to swerve aside for the need of a hundred or two dollars here and there that I could make by stopping to write this or that article." She implores Mr. Fields to "see if anything is due me on your accounts, as I have at this moment an especial pressure and it worries me to think how quickly I could earn a thousand dollars..." With a bustling household such as hers, those "tens of thousands" earned with *Uncle Tom's Cabin* (which represented a tidy sum in those days), were apparently not sufficient to bring complete ease.

Earning extra money on the side by writing might actually be more difficult today than it was in the nineteenth century. The array of paying outlets for writing has long since shrunk dramatically. Anyone who writes will relate to Stowe's quandary in the previous paragraph: how does one maintain the energy and find the time to do creative work while pursuing a necessary livelihood? A writing colleague of mine has steadfastly resisted getting a day job, and as a result, both her art and finances have suffered. Many of our esteemed predecessors had to find ways to be enterprising in tandem with working on preferred projects; often, an accommodating day job can be a splendid way to support a writing life.

HARRIET BEECHER STOWE: A WOMAN'S WORK IS NEVER DONE

 There is no doubt in my mind that our expenses this year will come to two hundred dollars, if not three, beyond our salary. We shall be able to come through, notwithstanding; but I don't want to feel obliged to work as hard every year as I have this. I can earn four hundred dollars a year by writing, but I don't want to feel that I must, and when weary with teaching the children, and tending the baby, and buying provisions, and mending dresses, and darning stockings, sit down and write a piece for some paper … I was just in some discouragement with regard to my writing; thinking that the editor of the "Era" was overstocked with contributors, and would not want my services another year, and lo! he sends me one hundred dollars, and ever so many good words with it. Our income this year will be seventeen hundred dollars in all, and I hope to bring our expenses within thirteen hundred.

— From a letter to her husband, 1850

NO LONGER POOR, NOT YET RICH

 You ask with regard to the remuneration which I have received for my work here in America. Having been poor all my life and expecting to be poor the rest of it, the idea of making money by a book which I wrote just because I couldn't help it, never occurred to me. It was therefore an agreeable surprise to receive ten thousand dollars as the first-fruits of three months' sale. I presume as much more is now due.

— From a letter to a fellow abolitionist
  (Eliza Cabot Follen), 1853

UNCLE TOM'S CAB

or,

LIFE AMONG THE

BY

RIET BEECHER STOW

VOL. II.

IXTIETH THOUS

BOSTON:
P. JEWETT &
CLEVELAND, OH
JEWETT, PROCTOR & WOR
1852.

UNCLE TOMS
CABIN

How quickly the minutes fly when you are writing to please your heart. I pity those who write for money or for fame. Money is debasing, and fame transitory and exacting. But for your own heart...Oh, what a difference!

— Anaïs Nin
The Early Diaries of Anaïs Nin
Entry dated October 1921

AH, YOUTH! HOW IDEALISTIC IT IS TO BE UNCONCERNED, LIKE THE young, passionate Anaïs Nin, with the intersection of art and commerce, and to create only to please your own heart. There's no shame in writing for personal pleasure if this is your true aim, or if you believe that focusing entirely on the creative process will be the surest path to your goals, whatever they may be.

Fast forward some twenty years from the quote at left, and Nin chafed at her financial discomfort : "I cannot make money. I'm a worker, I'm clever, I'm dexterous, I'm talented, yet I cannot make money." Still, her generosity impelled her to give what little funds she had to help her fellow artists, including her lover, Henry Miller. Not long after noting this lament in her diary, Nin decided she *did* want to be published, but no commercial publisher would take a risk on her collection of short stories, *Under a Glass Bell.* So in 1944, with her then-husband, Hugh Guiler, she founded Gemor Press for the purpose of printing the book. The desire to see one's words in print can sometimes overwhelm reason, as self-publishing tends to create more outgo than income.

In *A Room of One's Own,* Virginia Woolf pondered: "Why did men drink wine and women water? Why was one sex so prosperous and the other so poor? What effects does poverty have on fiction? What conditions are necessary for the creation of works of art?" These questions linger to this day, especially if we replace the word "fiction" with "writing." While it's safe to say that for many of those who love to write, the practice will be an avocation rather than a full-time, paid profession, there's no ignoring the fact that economic hardship has hampered many potentially brilliant writing careers. One notable example is Zora Neale Hurston. This talented African-American writer, whose work was so gutsy and daring, struggled constantly due to lack of steady income. She died impoverished and forgotten; fortunately, Alice Walker resuscitated her career. Hurston's books have sold in the millions posthumously, and she's celebrated and studied widely. Imagine what more she may have accomplished without lifelong money troubles.

Bringing thoughts of financial rewards to the desk may not inspire good writing; but neither does worry over how to pay bills. The Literary Ladies, each in their individual ways, and often after many years of effort, found a formula for merging creativity with commerce. It seems that for those who made it work particularly well, the key was acknowledging the role money played in their writing life, and taking ownership of their income and business affairs.

EDNA FERBER: MONEY GAINED, LOST, AND REGAINED

 Throughout the years of my writing life I had been thrifty and lavish at the same time. The thrift consisted of three very simple rules which I have observed all my life. I never bought anything for which I could not pay cash on the spot. I never borrowed a penny or owed a penny. I tried to put by at least something of each sum earned. I had seen the misery and fear that improvidence could cause. I wanted none of it.

Novels, plays, motion pictures, serializations, foreign rights had brought me enormous returns; at least, they seemed enormous to me. Part of this money I had, from time to time, invested as best I knew how, without speculation and without any desire to make money on the money itself. I knew that I could earn a living as long as I kept my health; I was strong, ambitious, I loved my work. I had tried to keep my life as simple as possible within the realm of comfort.

Now though all my energies seemed concentrated on finishing this book [*Cimarron*] one small still voice was whispering a warning. As I plodded on I looked about me uneasily. I know nothing (and knew nothing) of finance. Investments and investing bore me. The stock market is a mystery to my unmathematical mind. But certain fundamental truths have penetrated even my untechnical intelligence. One of them is this: a top-heavy structure, if piled higher, will tumble...

Ten days before the finish of *Cimarron* the stock market crashed. I lost more than everything I had saved. This should have depressed me very much indeed. It didn't. I wasn't disturbed for a moment — or for little more than a moment, at most. Money lost is money lost ... I went calmly on finishing my book, and when it was finished I found I had made a lot of money all over again. *Cimarron* was published serially; it was published as a novel and sold over 200,000 copies; it was made into a superb motion picture, the finest motion picture that has ever been made of any book of mine.

— *A Peculiar Treasure*, 1939

EDNA FERBER IS THE RARE AUTHOR FOR WHOM MAKING MONEY seemed almost easy. Nearly everything she did during her lifetime turned to gold. Single and childless, she devoted all her energies to her profession. She traveled extensively to research her panoramic novels, wrote or co-wrote the screenplay adaptations for eight of her novels (which became major Hollywood movies), and collaborated with George S. Kaufman on five plays that became huge Broadway hits in the 1920s and 1930s. She would be nearly as much a rarity in our time as she was in hers.

In 1959, Carson McCullers lamented, "Why does one write? Truly it is financially the most ill-rewarded occupation in the world. My lawyer has figured out how much I made from the book *The Member of the Wedding*, and it is, over the five years I worked on it, twenty-eight cents a day." (The better news is that McCullers subsequently made a fortune on the staged version of the book.) I know how she feels; I've been known to say I'm making "negative minimum wage" on certain projects.

If you were a creative dreamer back in the 1980s and 1990s, you may remember the book, *Do What You Love, the Money Will Follow,* by Marsha Sinetar. The book's advice holds up surprisingly well considering how the economy has shrunk since the go-go eighties and nineties. "The money will follow" means letting go of preconceived notions of success and expectations of instant gratification. It means accepting a waiting period that the author says requires "judgment, choice, and faith." But the most important part of "the money will follow," Sinetar writes, is "the ability to think well of ourselves, and our capabilities, even without money." What a comforting notion to consider for anyone who writes, whether you're anticipating that money will follow (soon or eventually), or if it's the furthest thing from your mind as your fingers hit the keyboard.

CHAPTER EIGHT | Farther Along the Path

*O*ne of the reviews says,
*"The book radiates happiness
and optimism." When I think
of the conditions of worry and
gloom and care under which
it was written I wonder at this
... I would not wish to darken
any other life — I want
instead to be a messenger of
optimism and sunshine ... It
is a joy to feel that my long
years of struggle and unaided
effort have been crowned
with success.*

— L.M. Montgomery
  From her journal,
  entry dated January 1910

A CASUAL POLL I CONDUCTED AMONG MY WRITING COLLEAGUES revealed that everyone who writes has at least fantasized about being published in some form or another, and that everyone who has been published dreams that their book (or books) will sell briskly. But it's also understood that writing, in its essence, isn't about publishing. At the risk of being obvious, writing truly is a journey, and a writer need not have any particular destination in sight. As you've read from the experiences of the Literary Ladies throughout the chapters, the journey can be one of self-discovery, finding a clear and true voice, shaking the foundations of culture, unleashing the imagination, disseminating fascinating information, or sharing a universal story.

All that being said, the publishing process is endlessly fascinating to those who write. Being farther along the path, as this chapter's title implies, means arriving at a place where your writing has an audience. This entails dealing with publicity (with all its ups and downs); handling criticism; continuing to work when the stakes are higher and there are suddenly others to please; and other issues that ensue once writing has crossed the boundary from private to public.

And for the very fortunate among the Literary Ladies, there was the richly deserved reaping of various honors and distinctions, as well as the ease that comes with financial rewards. One of those was Harriet Beecher Stowe, whose *Uncle Tom's Cabin* was the first book of fiction that became an international bestseller. This modest woman became a global literary star, fêted at home and abroad (while taking her share of lumps, as well). Her quotes at right encapsulate the highs and lows of the publishing experience, both of which she seemed to take in stride.

As they traveled farther along the writing path, none of the authors we've gotten to know in this book were content to rest on their laurels. "Great though it may be to publish, publishing is not the purpose of writing," wrote Brenda Ueland in *If You Want to Write*. "In the end, being published will not change your life, but writing will. If you are to be a writer who writes, you will never be finished. Stories may pass beneath your pen, or essays, poems, plays, books, fiction or nonfiction. Don't worry that you'll run out of ideas or subjects. You won't. Always, always there will be something more to write." How true — whether they lived long years or not, each of the Literary Ladies wrote nearly until they drew their last breaths. If nothing else, that's something worth aspiring to.

Harriet Beecher Stowe: "Who cares what the critics say?"

One hundred thousand copies of Dred sold in four weeks! After that who cares what critics say? Its success in England has been complete, so far as sale is concerned. It is very bitterly attacked, both from a literary and a religious point of view. The *Record* is down upon it with a cartload of solemnity; the *Athenaeum* with waspish spite; the *Edinburgh* goes out of its way to say that the author knows nothing of the society she describes; but yet it goes everywhere, is read everywhere, and Mr. Low says that he puts the hundred and twenty-fifth thousand to press confidently. The fact that so many good judges like it better than *Uncle Tom* is success enough.

— From a letter to her husband, September 1856

Worth all the suffering of writing

It is wonderful that people here* do not seem to get over *Uncle Tom* a bit. The impression seems fresh as if just published. How often have they said, "That book has revived the gospel among the poor of France; it has done more than all the books we have published put together ..." Is not this blessed, my dear husband? Is it not worth all the suffering of writing it?

—From a letter to her husband, November 1856
  * writing from Paris

CHARLOTTE BRONTË: NOTE TO CRITICS: BE GENTLE

 What will the critics of the monthly reviews and magazines be likely to see in *Jane Eyre* (if indeed they deign to read it), which will win from them even a stinted modicum of approbation? It has no learning, no research, it discusses no subject of public interest. A mere domestic novel will, I fear, seem trivial to men of large views and solid attachments.

— From a letter to her editor (W.S. Williams), October 1847

JUDGE ME AS AN AUTHOR ONLY, NOT AS A WOMAN

 To value praise or stand in awe of blame we must respect the source whence the praise and blame proceed, and I do not respect an inconsistent critic. He says, "If *Jane Eyre* be the production of a woman, she must be a woman unsexed."

In that case the book is an unredeemed error and should be unreservedly condemned. *Jane Eyre* is a woman's autobiography, by a woman it is professedly written. If it is written as no woman would write, condemn it with spirit and decision — say it is bad, but do not eulogise and then detract. I am reminded of *The Economist*. The literary critic of that paper praised the book if written by a man, and pronounced it "odious" if the work of a woman.

To such critics I would say, "To you I am neither man nor woman — I come before you as an author only. It is the sole standard by which you have a right to judge me — the sole ground on which I accept your judgment."

— From a letter to her editor (W.S. Williams), August 1849

AT THE DAWN OF THE PUBLICATION OF "JANE EYRE," CHARLOTTE Brontë worried that her book would receive no serious consideration at all. A classic case of "be careful what you wish for," her book became an immediate bestseller, and garnered all sorts of attention for its author, who was only known under her masculine pen name, Currer Bell. Rumors immediately began to swirl about the identity of the author of *Jane Eyre*. It was widely reviewed, though the results were not always pleasing to Brontë, whose defenses went up. Even a critic who wrote a complimentary review received a prickly response in writing from her. Once her identity as "Currer Bell" began to slip, she bristled when critics weighed the merits of the book on the basis of the gender of its author.

Wuthering Heights, her sister Emily's book, and *Agnes Gray,* by her sister Anne, were published a few months after *Jane Eyre,* though they'd been accepted before hers. More than the critiques of her own book, the reviews of her sisters' novels irked her: "They appeared at last. Critics failed to do them justice." More irritating yet was the rumor that the authors of *Wuthering Heights* and *Jane Eyre* were one and the same: "It was said that this was an earlier and ruder attempt of the same pen which had produced *Jane Eyre*," she wrote, "Unjust and grievous error! We laughed at it at first, but I deeply lament it now."

If such rumors could gain traction in the mid-1800s, consider how they can snowball in this age of what's so aptly called "the lawless Internet." In her memoir *The Opposite of Fate,* Amy Tan recounts her surprise at learning that she is the mother of two children, has won the Nobel Prize in Literature, lives in a mansion, and has taught poetry at a university in West Virginia, among other baseless myths soberly presented as facts. If Charlotte Brontë laughed at untruths about herself first and lamented them later, Tan seems to have taken the more sanity-preserving route, gathering up all the rumors and deflating them in one graceful, wry essay, and being done with them.

BACK IN THE DAY, WHEN BOOK REVIEWS RESIDED QUIETLY IN PRINT media, an author could consciously avoid reading reviews of her work. Unless a loud-mouthed aunt or neighbor broadcast the verdict, one could remain blissfully unaware of others' opinions. Carson McCullers said, "I never read my reviews. If they're good, they might give me the big-head, and if they are unfavorable, I would be depressed. So why bother?" Edna Ferber took a different view: "There are writers who say they pay no attention to reviews of their books, never read them, and don't care whether they're good or bad. I am not one of these. I do read them and I do care..."

Tears of joy or sorrow at reviews were usually shed as a private, matter between the author and her handkerchief or her journal, depending on which she preferred crying into. Today, if you're lucky to get reviewed at all, it's hard to avoid learning about them via Google alerts, e-mails from your editor or publicist, your social media networks, and all the various sources of Too Much Information. And this is aside from the praise or put-downs aimed at your book by online reader-reviewers, which you can easily avoid by simply not going to any of those sites if you have that sort of discipline (which, if you're like me, you probably don't).

No longer content with handkerchiefs or diaries, some authors now exact revenge on the public stage. Witness the now infamous Alice Hoffman incident. The author was displeased with a review of her 2009 novel, *The Story Sisters,* in her hometown (Boston) newspaper. She immediately took to Twitter, calling the reviewer "an idiot" and "a moron," and revealed the reviewer's e-mail address and home phone number. Her followers were urged to "tell her what u think of snarky critics." The publishing community as well as many readers were aghast at this behavior, even after Hoffman's tepid apology. Best to adopt Virginia Woolf's attitude, despite her discomfort with criticism, and "recover from praise and blame" quickly. Everyone whose writing goes public will experience both. Let them wash over you, glean what you can from each, and move on, as she did.

Virginia Woolf: "She Says I'm a Very Bad Writer"

What is the right attitude towards criticism? What ought I to feel and say when Miss B devotes an article in *Scrutiny* to attacking me? She is young, Cambridge, ardent. And she says I'm a very bad writer. Now I think the thing to do is to note the pith of what is said — that I don't think — than to use the little kick of energy which opposition supplies to be more vigorous oneself. It is perhaps true that my reputation will now decline. I shall be laughed at and pointed at... Of course, with my odd mixture of extreme rashness and modesty (to analyse roughly) I very soon recover from praise and blame. But I want to find out an attitude. The most important thing is not to think very much about oneself. To investigate candidly the charge; but not fussily, not very anxiously. On no account to retaliate by going to the other extreme — thinking too much. And now that thorn is out — perhaps too easily.

— *A Writer's Diary,* entry dated May 17, 1932

"'Time and Tide' says I'm a first rate novelist"

Time and Tide says I'm a first-rate novelist and a great lyrical poet. And I can already hardly read the reviews: but feel a little dazed, to think then it's not nonsense; it does make an effect...after all that agony, I'm free, whole; round: can go full ahead. And so stop this cry of content and sober joy.

— *A Writer's Diary*, entry dated March 12, 1937

Madeleine L'Engle:
"What review stays in your mind?"

 When we write and are published, we become naked before people ... it's hard for us to open ourselves to rebuff. I bleed from bad reviews, even though I have been very blessed in getting many more good reviews than bad reviews. But like every other writer I know, when you get ninety-nine good reviews and one bad review, what review stays in your mind? The bad one. And why? Because it awakens our own doubts. Did I really serve the work? Did I really hear it? Could she really be right and I haven't done it as I should have?

If you're going to write and be published, you've got to expect to have a few arrows thrown at you. They're going to hurt, and you're going to bleed. You're probably going to cry if you're like me. But that's just part of it and you have to learn.

— *Madeleine L'Engle Herself,* 2001

Say you've gotten a whole slew of great reviews and a tiny number of negative ones. Which ones are you most likely to remember (or more precisely, still be obsessing about) five years hence? Of course, it's the negative (and even the slightly negative) ones. The very doubts you think you've overcome once your work is in print are thus woken from their slumber. L'Engle doesn't shy away from describing the hurt that goes along with negative publicity, but she reminds us, always, to serve the work first.

Being a respected and renowned author is no defense against harsh reviews, now or in the past. Just the opposite is sometimes true; publishing success seems to bring out reviewers' sharpest pens. Annie Proulx, widely known for *The Shipping News* and the novella *Brokeback Mountain*, declared, "After things are published I never read them again. I never, ever read reviews." A good thing, perhaps, as reviews of a short story collection released after the acclaimed film version of *Brokeback Mountain* were mixed.

A *New York Times* review of Harriet Beecher Stowe's novel, *The Minister's Wooing* (1859), published just a few years after the triumph of *Uncle Tom's Cabin,* sniped afresh at the latter. The review panned her past and present work in one dismissive paragraph: "We never felt much sympathy for the extravagant admiration conferred on that novel specifically, and on the social justice and slavery themes in Stowe's work in general. To use novels as weapons of attack or defense is like giving foul blows in boxing. You may disable your antagonist, but you degrade yourself, and doubly degrade the supporters who applaud you." There's no way of knowing Stowe's reaction to this particular review, but it evidently didn't change the way she wrote or what she wrote about.

Edith Wharton advised: "If one has sought the publicity of print, and sold one's wares in the open market, one has sold to the purchasers the right to think what they choose about one's books; and the novelist's best safeguard is to put out of his mind the quality of praise or blame bestowed on him by reviewers and readers, and to write only for that dispassionate and ironic critic who dwells within the breast." With all due respect to the authors who say they ignore all reaction to their work, I simply don't think I could do this, though I can see the merit of not allowing others' opinions to influence one's efforts. Still, if I'm writing for others, I'm interested in reactions to the work, especially from readers. As for occasional sniping and sour grapes, that's why growing a tough hide is advisable. I can handle it, I think ...

My literary success puzzled and embarrassed my old friends far more than it impressed them, and in my own family it created a kind of constraint which increased with the years. None of my relations ever spoke to me of my books, either to praise or to blame — they simply ignored them; and among the immense tribe of my New York cousins, though it included many with whom I was on terms of affectionate intimacy, the subject was avoided as though it were a kind of family disgrace, which might be condoned but not be forgotten. Only one eccentric widowed cousin, living a life of lonely invalidism, turned to my novels for occasional distraction, and had the courage to tell me so.

At first I felt this indifference acutely; but now I no longer cared, for my recognition as a writer had transformed my life. I had made my own friends, and my books were beginning to serve as an introduction to my fellow-writers. But it was amusing to think that, whereas in London even my modest achievements would have opened many doors, in my native New York they were felt only as a drawback and embarrassment.

— *A Backward Glance,* 1934

WHEN HER FIRST NOVEL BECAME A BESTSELLER in 1905, Edith Wharton exulted to her publisher, Charles Scribner, "It is a very beautiful thought that 80,000 people should want to read *The House of Mirth,* and if the number should ascend to 100,000 I fear my pleasure would exceed the bounds of decency." How delighted she would be if the word reached her in the Great Beyond that *The House of Mirth* is still in print, as are *Ethan Frome, The Age of Innocence,* and many of her other titles. Fortunately, she enjoyed enough achievement in her lifetime to assuage the rebuff from those close to her, something that continued to be a sore point, illustrated by the passage at left.

Though it's wonderful to acknowledge the success reaped by such worthy role models as the Literary Ladies, in terms of accolades, literary prizes, and financial rewards, it's also worth considering what they gave as well as what they received. When writers succeed as resoundingly as they did, the pleasure of their creations ripples through countless generations (as, for example, Jane Austen's stories and characters have done, both in print and film). When Madeleine L'Engle won the National Humanities Medal, it not only vindicated her long years of struggle, but receiving it, among many other such honors, meant that she touched (and perhaps changed) the lives of countless others. Though Harriet Beecher Stowe's heart did little dances at the considerable earnings from her books, her letters indicate that it was the ability of *Uncle Tom's Cabin* to create a seismic shift in public awareness of slavery that gave her the most satisfaction. After doing well, Edith Wharton was inspired to do good; among other charitable work, she was named a *Chevalier* of the French Legion of Honor in 1916 for her tireless efforts on behalf of refugees during World War I.

Success is a concept that everyone must define for themselves, but one gauge that might be widely agreed on is the extent of one's ablity to give back, once the struggles have subsided.

After toiling so many years along the uphill road — always a hard one to women-writers — it is peculiarly grateful to me to find the way growing easier at last, with pleasant little surprises blossoming on either side, and the rough places made smooth by the courtesy and kindness of those who have proved themselves friends as well as publishers.

— Louisa May Alcott
   From a letter to
   her publisher,
   December, 1869

LOUISA MAY ALCOTT HAD ALREADY BECOME A famous author when she penned the response at right to a female reader asking for advice on achieving success as a writer. Alcott seemed rather smitten with her own narrative — one that has already become familiar to the readers of this book — and didn't mind repeating it for her own benefit and that of others.

Because her version of the path to success was ever paved with steady toil, any credit to her own talent was notably absent. She was by many standards an immensely gifted writer, and so, when she did become rich and famous, she had trouble adapting that image of herself with the one she was accustomed to: "It is droll, but I can't make the fortunate Miss A. [referring to herself] seem me, and only remember the weary years, the work, the waiting, and disappointment," she wrote to her sister Anna in 1870, "all that is forth in my mind; the other doesn't belong to me, and is a mistake somehow."

Reconciling the striving, hardworking version of oneself with a wealthy, bestselling one is a "problem" many writers would gladly grapple with, given the opportunity. Alcott's touching note to her publisher, at left, demonstrates gratitude for her success and a humble acceptance of all the pleasures it conferred. Despite her occasional grumbling, doing work she much preferred over all else made the sacrifices seem worthwhile, and when the rewards came, she truly appreciated them. Of course, it didn't hurt that her success allowed her to provide for those she loved.

Louisa May Alcott: No easy road to success

 I can only say to you as I do to the many young writers who ask for advice — There is no easy road to successful authorship; it has to be earned by long and patient labor, many disappointments, uncertainties and trials. Success is often a lucky accident, coming to those who may not deserve it, while others who do have to wait & hope till they have earned it. This is the best sort and the most enduring.

I worked for twenty years poorly paid, little known, and quite without any ambition but to eke out a living, as I chose to support myself and begin to do it at sixteen. This long drill was of use, and when I wrote "Hospital Sketches" by the beds of my soldier boys in the shape of letters home I had no idea that I was taking the first step toward what is called fame. It nearly cost me my life but I discovered the secret of winning the ear & touching the heart of the public by simply telling the comic & pathetic incidents of life.

"Little Women" was written when I was ill, and to prove that I could not write books for girls. The publisher thought it flat, so did I, and neither hoped much for or from it. We found out our mistake, and since then, though I do not enjoy writing "moral tales" for the young, I do it because it pays well.

But the success I value most was making my dear mother happy in her last years & taking care of my family. The rest soon grows wearisome & seems very poor beside the comfort of being an early Providence to those we love.

— From a letter to a reader, December 1878

A WRITER NEEDS TO BE COMFORTABLE, AT LEAST IN THEORY, WITH the idea of spending many quiet hours working alone. "There are days when solitude is a heady wine that intoxicates you with freedom," wrote Colette, "others when it is a bitter tonic, and still others when it is a poison that makes you beat your head against the wall." Occasional loneliness aside, creating a body of work is aided by being able to work solo, and this is usually fine and dandy with those who choose this vocation.

Once you publish and your work gains any sort of attention, the big adjustment for us solitary types is having to become a public person, at least in the aftermath of a book's publication. While laboring anonymously, many writers dream of doing radio shows, granting interviews, going on author tours, and above all, appearing on *Oprah* (though, by the time this book is in print, she will have retired her longtime talk show). If this becomes a reality, however, the opportunity to go public can induce sheer panic.

Willa Cather allegedly had a fierce love/hate relationship with the press. She courted fame in her youth, but claimed discomfort with it once it arrived. Yet unlike most of the other Literary Ladies, whose first-person musings in this collection come primarily from letters, journals, and memoirs, Cather's quotes came mainly from interviews she granted and public speeches she made. She also wrote many biographical sketches, press releases, and even semi-reviews in the third-person as a way to promote her work. Yet the more known she became, the more irritable she grew with loss of privacy.

For someone as ambivalent about publicity as Cather claimed to be, she seemed willing to grant scores of interviews, and judging by the vigor of her responses, she also seemed to enjoy holding forth on subjects dear to her heart. She gave dozens of speeches, many of which were transcribed for posterity. If the phrase had been invented in her heyday (in which the only forms of promotion available to authors were print media and lecturing), Cather would have been the model of a "media-savvy" author.

More than ever, publishers want authors who can spring into action as fully-formed media mavens. And that no longer means knowing a few local newspaper reporters or having a friend of a friend at *Vogue*. Publishers love authors who come with a solid platform, which might include, but isn't limited to, tons of fans and followers in the social media world, a popular blog, video channel, or podcast, and who are schooled in the techniques of networking in this virtual realm.

I can almost imagine Willa Cather conversing with the book-loving Oprah, these two dynamic women having a stimulating conversation about books, the writing life, inspiration, and discipline. But I can't picture her interacting with fans as some authors do today; she clearly wanted to be the one to call the shots when it came to how much she gave out to the press and public. And despite her generous outpouring of lectures and interviews, she guarded her privacy. At one point, while working on her next-to-last novel, *Lucy Gayheart,* Cather felt so besieged by the press, public, and Hollywood, that she shut her phone off during work hours and hired a secretary to pen impersonal responses to the many letters she received. She complained: "In this country a writer has to hide and lie and almost steal in order to get time to work — and peace of mind to work with."

To gain recognition for your work is a blessing. To achieve renown is a mixed blessing. Becoming a public person can be fun in small doses for those who can muster grace under pressure. Fifteen minutes of fame is something many writers would be willing to experience; but then it's back to the writing desk and into a tranquil harbor where our work can flourish.

IN HER OWN WAY, LUCY MAUD
Montgomery presaged the media-savvy
authors of today: she built a loyal following,
corresponded with swooning readers, and gave
them what she thought they wanted. When a
first book is such an immediate hit (as was *Anne
of Green Gables*), the publisher and public often
want more of the same, and the fortunate author,
wishing to build on her following, strives to oblige.

Though she complains of having to return to the
first novel's themes with her second as well as third books,
Montgomery treasured her popularity and strove to keep her
readers happy. She convinced herself that her fans would
accept nothing other than the formula that made her famous.
Though it's sometimes tricky to escape a genre in which one has
succeeded, it's not impossible. Montgomery managed to break
away from the beloved Anne after the fourth book in the series
(though she interspersed *The Story Girl* saga in between) and
created new characters. Emily (of the *Emily of the New Moon*
series) is an autobiographical character; and given the author's
perpetual angst, the story lines are darker and somewhat more
grim. Emily is a flawed but ultimately more "real" character
than the ebullient Anne. Years later, she happily revisited the
very grown-up version of Anne, her most iconic character.

Montgomery expressed mixed feelings about her fame ("I
am pestered with letters from tourists who are holidaying on
the Island who say they have read my book and want to 'meet'
me ... I don't want to be 'met,'" she griped in a letter), but still
wished to please her readers, who remained satisfied with her
subsequent works, despite her fears. It was she alone who
believed that they wouldn't tolerate change; once she realized
her error, she wrote as she pleased, always from the heart, and
her fans were all too happy to follow along.

L.M. Montgomery:
When your public clamors for more

I finished my second "Anne" book the other day and am now revising it and later on will have to typewrite it. I began it last winter at the request of the publishers, supposing I'd have plenty of time to do it in. But since the first one has caught on they have been urging me to have it ready by October. As a result I have been writing furiously all through this hot summer. For this reason I don't think the book is as good — comparatively speaking — as the first. But I may not be able to judge — I feel so soaked and saturated with "Anne" that I'm sick of the sound of her name.

— From a letter to a friend (G.B. MacMillan), 1909

"They will not tolerate a change"

I am now girding up the loins to begin a third "Anne" book. This is to be written to satisfy my publisher and public, not myself. I am very reluctant to begin it. It seems so hard to get back into the atmosphere of Anne — like putting on a dress worn years ago, which, no matter how beautiful still, is something I have outgrown and find out of fashion with my later development. However, I shall make the attempt in order to make peace for myself. I fear that I must henceforth be a slave to the style that the public have learned to expect from me. They will not tolerate a change. And I should like to try my hand at a different type of book. Someday I shall — when I have made enough money to be independent of the public taste.

— From a letter to a friend (G.B. MacMillan), 1914

JANE AUSTEN: THE INNOCENCE OF A "DARLING CHILD"

 I want to tell you that I have got my own darling child from London*...I must confess that I think her [Elizabeth Bennett] as delightful a creature as ever appeared in print, and how I shall be able to tolerate those who do not like her at least I do not know.

—Jane Austen, from a letter to her sister Cassandra, 1813
  *Referring to *Pride and Prejudice*

SELF-CONSCIOUSNESS SETS IN

 I must make use of this opportunity, to thank you, dear Sir, for the very high praise you bestow on my other novels. I am too vain to wish to convince you that you have praised them beyond their merits. My greatest anxiety at present is that this fourth work should not disgrace what was good in the others. But on this point I will do myself the justice to declare that, whatever may be my wishes for its success, I am strongly haunted with the idea that to those readers who have preferred "Pride and Prejudice" it will appear inferior in wit, and to those who have preferred "Mansfield Park" inferior in good sense.

—Jane Austen, from a letter to a librarian, 1815

THERE'S NOTHING LIKE THE SHEER INNOCENCE of writing your first major book-length work of fiction or nonfiction. Unless you're writing it for a master's thesis or in full view of your writer's group, you're unencumbered by anyone looking over your shoulder.

If you're fortunate enough to have that book published, everything changes. The stakes are higher, as are expectations, not the least of which, your own. You suddenly feel self-conscious, with real or imagined onlookers peering over your shoulder. I'm not sure which is harder to follow: a fair-to-middling seller or an outright flop (which makes it tougher to get a second chance). Trickier still is figuring out what to do after a rare, resounding success that comes early in one's career.

Amy Tan devoted an entire chapter to "Angst and the Second Book" in her memoir, *The Opposite of Fate*, that's both hilarious and harrowing. She recounts being asked at a panel discussion, "How does it feel to have written your best book first?" She's reminded more than once that she'll have a hell of a time following her own act. This set in motion such an avalanche of false starts that the second book she completed was actually the result of her eighth attempt.

Jane Austen was just as concerned as any previously published author that she would produce a book that "should not disgrace what was good in the others." All the pressure to outdo oneself with each successive publication seems largely self-imposed. No one cares more than you whether your second book is better than your first (well, your publisher cares, though not as much as you do), or if your ninth book is better than your eighth. Barbara Kingsolver provides the only good solution to this: "Close the door. Write with no one looking over your shoulder. Don't try to figure out what other people want to hear from you; figure out what you have to say. It's the one and only thing you have to offer."

Of course a second work has occupied my thoughts much. I think it would be premature in me to undertake a serial now — I am not yet qualified for the task: I have neither gained a sufficiently firm footing with the public nor do I possess sufficient confidence in myself.

— Charlotte Brontë
From a letter to her publisher, 1847

WHEN I BEGAN A GRADUATE ART PROGRAM SOME years ago, I was told that students frequently embark on their studies with a particular objective in mind and emerge having accomplished something unexpected — and quite surprising to themselves. This was brought to my mind when I learned of the evolution of Anaïs Nin's celebrated *Diary* series. In the first chapter, Becoming a Writer, we learned that for Nin, writing was as essential as breathing, and this need inspired her diaries. What started as a one woman's personal quest for identity and meaning ended by becoming a series of published books that delved into universal issues affecting women in all walks of life. Her diaries became touchstones for a generation of women, and Nin herself became a feminist icon.

By the standards of today's confessional media, Nin's frank writings may no longer seem as revolutionary as they did just a generation ago (though the fact that she maintained two marriages simultaneously continues to astonish). In the final volume of the *Diary of Anaïs Nin* (*Volume Seven*, 1966–1974), she delights in sharing snippets from the countless letters of gratitude she received from women everywhere, in all walks of life: "The diaries wakened me, made me relive my life, enjoy it, and find new aspects to dream about; you gave me a second life." "My world is richer because you have given me yours." "You taught me to be a woman of tenderness, affection and independence." "Your writings, your honesty, helped me accept myself as a person, a woman, an artist."

This encapsulates, in the end, what writing is for — it's a way to know ourselves and make sense of our individual journey, and in the process create something that resonates with others. Books that become classics, whether fiction or nonfiction, highlight the common threads of experience, no matter when or where they're set. Anaïs Nin started by examining her own life, and ended by speaking for masses of women in their quest for self-knowledge and the courage to grow.

ANAÏS NIN: FROM THE PERSONAL TO THE UNIVERSAL

 Having been told so often how wrong it is to write about one's self — how I should take the self out of the *Diary* — I never expected the consequences. Because I gave of myself, many women felt I spoke for them, liberated them from secrecy and reticence. I did not expect to get letters from women working in offices, on farms, married and lonely in little towns, nurses, librarians, students, runaways, dropouts, pregnant women without husbands, women in the middle of a divorce. Suddenly I was discovering a world.

The dominant theme of the letters was loneliness and lack of confidence in whatever the writers undertook. The miracle was that my diary made them eloquent, confessional ... I discovered women with talents never used before. One woman sent me her first drawing made after reading the *Diary*. The *Diary* cured depression, opened secret chambers.

There was no ego in the *Diary*, there was only a voice which spoke for thousands, made links, bonds, friendships. All the clichés about self-absorption were destroyed. There was no one self. We were all one. The more I developed my self, the less mine it became. If all of us were willing to expose this self, we would feel neither alone nor unique. I was so tired of the platitudes hurled at me. The two most misinterpreted words in the world: narcissism and ego. The simple truth was that some of us recognized the need to develop, grow, expand — occupations which are the opposite of those two words. To desire to grow means you are not satisfied with the self as it is, and the ego is exacting, not indulgent.

— *The Diary of Anaïs Nin, Volume Seven,* 1966–1974

Virginia Woolf:
Write "for the good of the world"

I would ask you to write all kinds of books, hesitating at no subject however trivial or how vast. By hook or by crook, I hope you will possess yourselves of money enough to travel and to idle, to contemplate the future or the past of the world, to dream over books and loiter at street corners and let the line of thought dip deep into the stream. For I am by no means confining you to fiction. If you would please me — and there are thousands like me — you would write books of travel and adventure, and research and scholarship, and history and biography, and criticism and philosophy and science. By so doing you will certainly profit the art of fiction. For books have a way of influencing each other.

Fiction will be much the better for standing cheek by jowl with poetry and philosophy. Moreover, if you consider any great figure of the past, like Sappho, like the Lady Murasaki, like Emily Brontë, you will find she is an inheritor as well as an originator, and has come into experience because women have come to the habit of writing naturally; so that even as a prelude to poetry such activity on your part would be invaluable ...

Thus when I ask you to write more books I am urging you to do what will be for your good and for the good of the world at large.

— *A Room of One's Own,* 1929

SO MANY PEOPLE WANT TO WRITE — AND LOVE TO WRITE — BECAUSE it's so eminently approachable, and so intertwined with the love of reading. It's one of the most democratic of arts, and because of that, has the richest legacy of female participation. I've long fantasized about being able to play Irish fiddle (why this is so is anyone's guess), but I'd have to buy an instrument (no small investment) and take many years of lessons before anything sounding remotely like music emerged. The prospect is overwhelming, so in the end I won't do it. But anyone can take a pen to paper and see words form sentences and reflect thoughts, whether such efforts are humble or exalted — today, not years from now.

The act of writing is simple in and of itself, but the endless possibilities it offers are what makes it so compelling. It's a yielding art, conforming itself to whatever niche — large or small — we wish to give it in our lives.

I could find no more fitting farewell for this collection than the passage at left. Virginia Woolf encouraged women to write about whatever fascinated them, and to dare to be dreamers and creators. Aside from fiction, nonfiction, and poetry, as she suggests, there are also essays, articles, song lyrics, screenplays, blog posts, and journal entries to pour one's heart into. By keeping words flowing, we can pay homage to the Literary Ladies in this book, as well as all the other women writers who have paved the way.

Sources, Notes, and Acknowledgments

Alcott, Louisa May

— *Alternative Alcott,* edited by Elaine Showalter. New Brunswick, NJ: Rutgers University Press, 1988

— *Little Women Abroad: The Alcott Sisters' Letters from Europe, 1870–1871,* edited by Daniel Shealy.
    Athens, GA: The University of Georgia Press, 2008

— *Louisa May Alcott: Her Life, Letters, and Journals,* edited by Ednah D. Cheney. Boston:
    Little, Brown and Co., 1889

— *The Selected Letters of Louisa May Alcott,* with an introduction by Madeleine B. Stern, edited by Joel Myerson
    and Daniel Shealy. NY: Little, Brown and Co., 1987

Austen, Jane

— *A Memoir of Jane Austen,* by James Edward Austen-Leigh (her nephew). London: MacMillan and Co., Ltd.
    NY: The MacMillan Co., 1869, 1906

— *The Bedside, Bathtub, & Armchair Companion to Jane Austen,* by Carol J. Adams, Douglas Buchanan, and
    Kelly Gesch. The Continuum International Publishing Group, Inc., 2008

— *Jane Austen and Her Times,* by Geraldine Edith Mitton. NY: G.P. Putnam's, 1905

— *The Illustrated Letters of Jane Austen,* edited by Penelope Hughes-Hallet. NY: Clarkson Potter, Inc., 1996

— *Letters of Jane Austen: Selected from the Compilation of her Great Nephew, Edward, Lord Brabourne,* edited by Susan Coolidge.
    London: Roberts Bros., 1892

Brontë, Charlotte

— *Biographical Notice of Ellis and Acton Bell,* by Charlotte Brontë, from the combined first edition of *Wuthering Heights*
    and *Agnes Grey* (by Emily and Anne Brontë, respectively). London: Smith, Elder, and Co., 1850 edition

— *The Brontës: Life and Letters,* edited by Clement King Shorter. NY: Charles Scribner's Sons, 1908

— *The Brontës: Their Lives, Friendships and Correspondence in Four Volumes,* Volume II, 1844–1849. Oxford: Shakespeare Head
    Press, Basil Blackwell; and Boston and NY: Houghton Mifflin Co., 1933

— *The Letters of the Brontës: A Selection,* edited by Muriel Spark. Norman, OK: University of Oklahoma Press, 1954

— *The Life of Charlotte Brontë,* by Elizabeth Cleghorn Gaskell. London: Smith, Elder, and Co., 1857

— *Wuthering Heights,* with an introduction by Pauline Nestor. NY: Penguin Books, 2003

Cather, Willa

— *Willa Cather in Person: Interviews, Speeches, and Letters,* selected and edited by L. Brent Bohlke. Archive at
    http://cather.unl.edu/index.bohlke.html, and book: Lincoln, NE: University of Nebraska Press, 1986

— *Willa Cather Remembered,* edited by Bohlke, Brent, and Hoover, Sharon.
    Lincoln, NE: University of Nebraska Press 2002

Ferber, Edna

— *A Kind of Magic,* by Edna Ferber. NY: Doubleday & Co., 1963

— *A Peculiar Treasure,* by Edna Ferber. NY: Doubleday, Doran & Co., 1939

L'Engle, Madeleine

— *A Circle of Quiet,* by Madeleine L'Engle. NY: Farrar, Straus, Giroux, 1972

— *Madeleine L'Engle Herself: Reflections on a Writing Life,* by Madeleine L'Engle, compiled by Carole F. Chase. NY: WaterBrook Multnomah, an imprint of the Crown Publishing Group, a division of Random House, Inc., 2001

— *Walking on Water: Reflections on Faith and Art,* by Madeleine L'Engle. NY: WaterBrook Multnomah, an imprint of the Crown Publishing Group, a division of Random House, Inc., 2001

— *A Wrinkle in Time,* by Madelein L'Engle (originally published in 1962). Paperback edition, NY: Bantam Doubleday Dell, 1998

Montgomery, L.M. (Lucy Maud)

— *Anne of Avonlea,* by L.M. Montgomery. Boston: L.C. Page and Co., 1909

— *The Green Gables Letters: from L.M. Montgomery to Ephraim Weber 1905–1909,* edited by Wilfred Eggleston. Toronto, Canada: Ryerson, Ltd., 1960

— *My Dear Mr. M.: Letters to G.B. MacMillan,* edited by Francis W.P. Bolger and Elizabeth R. Epperly. Toronto, Canada: McGraw-Hill Ryerson, Ltd., 1981

— *The Selected Journals of L.M. Montgomery, Volumes I–V,* edited by Mary Rubio and Elizabeth Waterston. Toronto, Canada: Oxford University Press, 1985–1992

— *Looking for Anne of Green Gables,* by Irene Gammel. NY: St. Martin's Press, NY © 2008

— *Writing a Life: L.M. Montgomery* by Mary Rubio and Elizabeth Waterston. Toronto: ECW Press, 1995

Nin, Anais

— *The Early Diaries of Anais Nin, Volume 2, 1920–1923.* NY: Harcourt Brace Jovanovich, 1982

— *The Diary of Anaïs Nin, Volume Seven, 1966–1974.* NY: Harcourt Brace Jovanovich, 1980

— *In Favor of the Sensitive Man and Other Essays* by Anaïs Nin. NY: Harcourt Brace Jovanovich, 1976

— *A Woman Speaks: The Lectures, Seminars, and Interviews of Anais Nin.* Chicago, IL: The Swallow Press, Inc., 1975

Sand, George

— *George Sand, Correspondance,* 25 volumes, edited by Georges Lubin, Paris: Garnier Freres, 1964–1995

— *Letters of George Sand, Volume 1,* translated and edited by Raphael Ledos de Beaufort.
   London: Ward and Downey, 1886

— *The George Sand–Gustave Flaubert Letters,* translated by Aimee L. McKenzie. NY: Boni & Liveright, Inc., 1921

— *The Intimate Journal of George Sand,* edited and translated by Marie Jenney Howe. NY: The John Day Co., 1929

Stowe, Harriet Beecher

— *Crusader in Crinoline: The Life of Harriet Beecher Stowe,* by Robert Forrest Wilson. Philadelphia and London:
   J.B. Lippincott Co., 1941

— *Harriet Beecher Stowe's Hartford Home* (pamphlet). Hartford, CT: Harriet Beecher Stowe Center, 2008

— *Life of Harriet Beecher Stowe, compiled from her Letters and Journals,* by her son Charles Edward Stowe. Boston:
   Houghton Mifflin and Company, 1889

— *Life and Letters of Harriet Beecher Stowe,* edited by Annie Fields. Boston and NY: Houghton, Mifflin
   and Company, 1897

Wharton, Edith

— *A Backward Glance.* NY and London: D. Appleton-Century Co., 1934

— *Edith Wharton: An Extraordinary Life, by* Eleanor Dwight. NY: Harry N. Abrams, 1999

— *The Letters of Edith Wharton,* edited by R.W.B. Lewis and Nancy Lewis. NY: Charles Scribner's sons, 1988

Woolf, Virginia

— *A Room of One's Own,* by Virginia Woolf (Fountain Press, 1929). NY: Harcourt, Inc., 1929

— "Women and Fiction," essay by Virginia Woolf, 1929

— *The Death of the Moth and Other Essays* by Virginia Woolf (Hogarth Press, 1942). NY: Harcourt, Brace and Co., 1942

— *The Letters of Virginia Woolf, Volumes I–III,* edited by Nigel Nicolson and Joanne Trautman Banks.
   NY: Harcourt, Brace, Jovanovich, 1975

— *A Writer's Diary: Being Extracts from the Diary of Virginia Woolf,* edited by Leonard Woolf.
   NY: Harcourt, Brace, and Co., NY, 1953, 1954

— *The Letters of Vita Sackville-West to Virginia Woolf,* edited by Louise DeSalvo and Mitchell A. Leaska.
   NY: William Morrow and Co., Inc., 1985

— *Virginia Woolf: A Biography, Volume 1,* by Quentin Bell. NY: Harcourt Jovanovich, 1972

Additional sources

Baudelaire, Charles. *My Heart Laid Bare,* edited by Peter Quennell, translated by Norman Cameron. London: Weidenfeld & Nicolson, 1950

Braxton, Joan. *Maya Angelou's I Know Why the Caged Bird Sings: A Casebook.* NY: Oxford University Press, 1998

Colette. *The Evening Star: Recollections* (original French edition published in 1946). Indianapolis and NY: The Bobbs-Merrill Co., Inc., 1973

Dally, Peter. *The Marriage of Heaven and Hell: Manic Depression and the Life of Virginia Woolf.* NY: St. Martin's Griffin, 2001

Dillard, Annie. *The Writing Life.* NY: Harper & Row, 1989

Lamott, Anne. *Bird by Bird: Some Instructions on Writing and Life.* NY: Anchor, 1995

Goldberg, Natalie. *Long Quiet Highway: Waking Up in America.* NY: Bantam, 1993

Hurston, Zora Neale. *Dust Tracks on a Road: An Autobiography.* Philadelphia: J.B. Lippincott, 1942

Jackson, Shirley. *Come Along with Me.* NY: Viking Press, 1968

Mansfield, Katherine. *The Letters of Katherine Mansfield, Volume II,* 1929

McCullers, Carson. *Illumination and Night Glare: The Unfinished Autobiography of Carson McCullers,* edited by Carlos L. Dews. Madison, WI: The University of Wisconsin Press, 1999

McCullers, Carson. Article, "The Flowering Dream," *Esquire,* December 1959

Moers, Ellen. *Literary Women.* NY: Doubleday & Co, Garden City, 1976

Morahan, Shirley. *A Woman's Place: Rhetoric and Readings for Composing Yourself and Your Prose.* Albany, NY: SUNY Press, 1981

Moulton, Louise Chandler (essay on LMA by) *Our Famous Women: An Authorized Record of the Lives and Deeds of Distinguished American Women of our Times.* Hartford, CT: A.D. Worthington, 1884

O'Connor, Flannery. *The Habit of Being,* edited by Sally Fitzgerald. NY: Farrar, Straus, Giroux, 1979

Olsen, Tillie. *Silences.* NY: Delacorte Press/Seymour Lawrence, 1978

Plath, Sylvia. *The Journals of Sylvia Plath,* edited by Frances McCullough; Ted Hughes, consulting editor. NY: Dial Press, 1982

Plath, Sylvia. *Letters Home: Correspondence 1950-1963.* NY: Harper & Row, 1975

Porter, Katherine Anne. *The Paris Review Interviews,* interview by Barbara Thompson, 1963

Porter, Katherine Anne. *Katherine Anne Porter Conversations,* edited by Joan Givner. Jackson, MS: University Press of Mississippi, 1987

Rawlings, Marjorie Kinnan. *The Uncollected Writings of Marjorie Kinnan Rawlings,* edited by Rodger L. Tarr and Brent E. Kinser. Gainseville, FL: University Press of Florida, 2007

Sackville-West, Vita. *Twelve Days.* Garden City, NY: Doubleday, Doran 1928

See, Carolyn. *Making a Literary Life: Advice for Writers and Other Dreamers.* NY: Random House, 2002

Sinetar, Marsha. *Do What You Love, the Money Will Follow: Discovering Your Right Livelihood.* NY: Dell,1989

Sternburg, Janet. *The Writer on Her Work, Volume 1.* NY: W.W. Norton and Company, revised edition, 2000

Tan, Amy. *The Opposite of Fate: Memories of a Writing Life.* NY: Penguin, 2003

Tarr, Rodger L. editor. *Max & Marjorie:The Correspondence between Maxwell E. Perkins and Marjorie Kinnan Rawlings.* Gainesville, FL: The University Press of Florida, 1999

Ueland, Brenda. *If You Want to Write: A Book About Art, Independence, and Spirit.* NY: G.P Putnam's Sons, 1938; Saint Paul, MN: Graywolf Press, 1987

Van Gelder, Robert. *Writers and Writing.* NY: Charles Scribner's Sons, 1946

Welty, Eudora. *The Paris Review Interviews: The Art of Fiction No. 47,* interview with Linda Kuehl, 1972

For easy identification in the sources section that follows, here is a key to the most frequently cited books:

ABG— *A Backward Glance* (Edith Wharton)

ACQ— *A Circle of Quiet* (Madeleine L'Engle)

AKOM— *A Kind of Magic* (Edna Ferber)

AMOJA— *A Memoir of Jane Austen*

APT— *A Peculiar Treasure* (Edna Ferber)

AROO—*A Room of One's Own* (Virginia Woolf)

AWD— *A Writer's Diary: Being Extracts from the Diary of Virginia Woolf*

EDAN— *The Early Diaries of Anais Nin*

GSC— *George Sand, Correspondance*

GS-GFL— *The George Sand—Gustave Flaubert Letters*

IYWTW— *If You Want to Write*

LGS— *Letters of George Sand*

LMA: HLLJ— *Louisa May Alcott: Her Life, Letters, and Journals*

LOHBS— *Life of Harriet Beecher Stowe*

LOCB— *The Life of Charlotte Brontë*

LOJA— *Letters of Jane Austen*

LOTB— *The Letters of the Brontés: A Selection*

LOVW— *Letters of Virginia Woolf*

SJLMM— *The Selected Journals of L.M. Montgomery*

SLLMA— *The Selected Letters of Louisa May Alcott*

TBLL— *The Brontës: Life and Letters*

TBTLFC— *The Brontës: Their Lives, Friendships and Correspondence in Four Volumes*

WAL— *Writing a Life* (L.M. Montgomery)

WCIP— *Willa Cather in Person: Interviews, Speeches, and Letters*

All unattributed images are stock photos, public domain, or from the author's own collection of ephemera.

Prologue

Page 9

Photo of Edith Wharton courtesy of Beineke Library, Yale University, Watkins / Loomis Agency, and the estate of Edith Wharton

Introduction

Page 13

Photo of Louisa May Alcott courtesy of New York Public Library

Drawing of Jane Austen courtesy of Wikimedia Commons

Drawing of Charlotte Brontë by George Richmond (ca. 1850) courtesy of Wikimedia Commons

Page 14

Photo of Willa Cather courtesy of New York Public Library

Photo of Edna Ferber courtesy of New York Public Library

Photo of Madeleine L'Engle courtesy of Wheaton College Archives & Special Collections

Page 15
Photo of L.M. Montgomery courtesy of Archival and Special Collections, University of Guelph Library, Guelph, Ontario, Canada

Photo of Anaïs Nin courtesy of Elsa Dorfman under the GNU Free Documentation License

Photo of George Sand courtesy of Wikimedia Commons

Photo of Harriet Beecher Stowe courtesy of The Harriet Beecher Stowe Center, Hartford, CT

Photo of Edith Wharton courtesy of the New York Public Library, Watkins / Loomis Agency, and the estate of Edith Wharton

Photo of Virginia Woolf courtesy of Wikimedia Commons

Page 17
Each person's method ... LMA: HLLJ

A woman writer... Sternburg, Janet. *The Writer on Her Work, Volume 1*

Chapter One
page 18
Photo courtesy of Sky Blue Press, Santa Fe, NM

Page 19
I believe I... EDAN

Page 21
I am more than ever... LGS

Page 22
Perhaps it is just as well... Hurston, Zora Neale. *Dust Tracks on a Road: An Autobiography*

Page 23
One writes for all the world... GS-GFL

Photo of Anaïs Nin courtesy of Sky Blue Press, Santa Fe, NM

Page 24
No two writers could be more ... AMOJA

Each writer equally resisted ... AMOJA

Page 25
I begin already... LOJA

It is evident that... LOCB

Page 26
I was married ... LOHBS

Photo of Harriet Beecher Stowe courtesy of New York Public Library, New York, NY

Photo of envelope with scenes from *Uncle Tom's Cabin* courtesy of The Harriet Beecher Stowe Center, Hartford, CT

Page 27
Now, Hattie, if I could ... LOHBS

Page 28
Photo of LMA courtesy of Wikimedia Commons

Page 29
Photo of LMM courtesy of Archival and Special Collections, University of Guelph Library, Guelph, Ontario, Canada

Page 31
January, 1862 — E.P. Peabody ... LMA:HLLJ

Photo of LMA courtesy of Wikimedia Commons

Page 33
I was contented enough with ... ABG

Page 34
Without passion, one writes ... Mansfield, Katherine. *The Letters of Katherine Mansfield*

It is necessary to write ... Sackville-West, Vita. *Twelve Days*

Chapter Two
Page 36
Photo of Willa Cather courtesy of the Willa Cather Foundation, Red Cloud, NE

Page 37
The business of writing is a ... WCIP

Page 39
When I was in college I ... WCIP

Page 39, continued
Photo of Willa Cather courtesy of the Willa Cather
Foundation, Red Cloud, NE

Page 40
When I was in college and ... WCIP

In Alexander's Bridge I was ... WCIP

Photo of Willa Cather courtesy of the Willa Cather
Foundation, Red Cloud, NE

Page 41
Every time Isabel Allende ... Lamott, Anne. *Bird by Bird*

Every dawning talent has to ... *The Letters of Edith Wharton*

Since we must and do ... Welty, Eudora. From an essay
"Words into Fiction," 1965

Photo courtesy of Beineke Library, Yale University,
Watkins / Loomis Agency, and the estate of Edith
Wharton

Page 42
The young writer must learn ... WCIP

Is not the real experience ... LOTB

Photo of Charlotte Brontë courtesy of Wikimedia
Commons

Page 43
Up to that time I had planned ... WCIP

Page 44
O why do I ever let ... LOVW

Photo of Virginia Woolf and her father courtesy of
Wikimedia Commons

Page 45
My writing makes me tremble ... LOVW

I will offer some explanation ... LOVW

Page 47
Photo of Edna Ferber courtesy of Appleton Public
Library; background art courtesy of Wikimedia
Commons

Page 49
My methods of work are ... SLLMA

Page 53
February, 1861. — Another turn at ... LMA:HLLJ

Background photo of Orchard House courtesy of
Daderot under the GNU Free Documentation License

Page 54
Photo of Edith Wharton courtesy of Beineke Library,
Yale University, Watkins / Loomis Agency, and the
estate of Edith Wharton

Page 55
Photo of Edith Wharton courtesy of Beineke Library,
Yale University, Watkins / Loomis Agency, and the
estate of Edith Wharton

Chapter Three
Page 56
Photo of Edna Ferber courtesy of
New York Public Library

Page 58
Edna Ferber postage stamps, USPS 2002

Page 61
Photo of Madeleine L'Engle courtesy of Wheaton
College Archives & Special Collections

Page 62
The fact that there are men... Baudelaire, Charles.
My Heart Laid Bare

How the devil did George Sand ... Colette,
The Evening Star

Page 63
While you are running around ... GS-GFL

Portait of George Sand courtesy of Wikimedia
Commons

For the present I am ... LGS

Page 64
I didn't have any particular gift ... Nin, Anaïs.
A Woman Speaks

Photo of Anaïs Nin by Elsa Dorfman courtesy of
Wikimedia Commons

Page 65
I love to write for the sake of ... Porter, Katherine
Anne. *The Paris Review Interviews*

Page 66
Miss Cather works but three hours ... WCIP

I write fast, having ... *The Green Gables Letters: from L.M.
Montgomery to Ephraim Weber 1905–1909*

Page 67
I work from two and a half ... WCIP

I used to write from morning ... SLLMA

Page 68
I have had a hard time ... SJLMM

Page 69
To work in silence and ... Bohlke, Brent, and Hoover,
Sharon. *Willa Cather Remembered*

Page 69, continued
Photo of LMM courtesy of Archival and Special
Collections, University of Guelph Library, Guelph,
Ontario, Canada

Page 70
People have writer's block .... Anna Quidlen in an
Amazon.com exclusive essay

If I have a dry spell ... Plath, Sylvia. *Letters Home:
Correspondence 1950–1963*

Page 71
When you plan such a huge ... IYWTW

I make writing as much... Braxton, Joan. *Maya Angelou's
I Know Why the Caged Bird Sings: A Casebook*

Chapter Four
Page 72
Photo of Virginia Woolf courtesy of Wikimedia
Commons

Page 73
Outwardly, what is simpler than ... Woolf, Virginia. *The
Death of the Moth and Other Essays*

Page 74
I had believed that established ... From a 1936 letter
from Margaret Mitchell to Stark Young, drama critic
at *The New Republic*

I assure you, all my novels ... LOVW

Photo, VW's British passport, 1923

Page 76
Unattributed photo of Leonard and Virginia Woolf

Page 77
Virginia's need to write was ... Dally, Peter. *The
Marriage of Heaven and Hell: Manic Depression and the Life of
Virginia Woolf*

Any day you open it to ... Welty, Eudora. Interview,
The Paris Review Interviews: The Art of Fiction No. 47

Page 78
Is it better to be extremely ... Sackville-West, Vita.
The Letters of Vita Sackville-West to Virginia Woolf

Pages 78–79
Background photos Photo courtesy of MacIntosh &
Otis, Inc. and the Estate of Madeleine L'Engle

Page 80
I never expected any sort... *Counterpoint,* interview with
Roy Newquist. Chicago: Rand McNally, 1964

Photo of Edna Ferber courtesy of The Library of
Congress

Page 82
Photo of George Sand by Félix Nadar courtesy of
Wikimedia Commons

As for my frenzy for work ... GS-GFL

Page 84
I think I may boast myself to be ... AMOJA

Page 85
The work is rather too light ... Mitton, Geraldine
Edith. *Jane Austen and Her Times.*

Portrait of Jane Austen courtesy of Wikimedia
Commons

Page 86
I can work indefatigably … TBLL

Page 88
Edith Wharton postage stamp, USPS

Page 89
I feel that I have no pretensions … *Max & Marjorie: The Correspondence between Maxwell E. Perkins and Marjorie Kinnan Rawlings*

After all, one know one's weak … *The Letters of Edith Wharton*

Photo of Edith Wharton courtesy of Beineke Library, Yale University, Watkins / Loomis Agency, and the estate of Edith Wharton

Chapter 5
Page 91
Photo courtesy of The Harriet Beecher Stowe Center, Hartford

Our children are just coming … LOHBS

Page 93
To be 29 & unmarried … Bell, Quentin. *Virginia Woolf: A Biography*

As for the choice between… WCIP

Photo of Willa Cather courtesy of the Willa Cather Foundation, Red Cloud, NE

Page 95
Creating a story is like … *The Bookman.* NY: Dodd Mead, and Co., 1914

Page 96
If I am to write … LOHBS

Photo courtesy of Wikimedia Commons

Page 97
I wrote what I did … *Harriet Beecher Stowe's Hartford Home*

To make this whole nation feel … LOHBS

As long as the baby sleeps … LOHBS

I have determined not to be a mere … Wilson, Forrest. *Crusader in Crinoline*

Page 98
The habits of a lifetime … Olson, Tillie. *Silences*

Page 99
We have had terrible weather… LOHBS

Since I began this note … LOHBS

Page 100
Self-abnegation is a noble thing … From a letter to a reader, Henry W. and Albert A. Berg Collection, New York Public Library

Page 101
She is a happy woman … LMA: HLLJ

I am more than half-persuaded … Moulton, Louise Chandler (essay). *Our Famous Women*

Page 103
And now I am very old … *The Intimate Journal of George Sand*

Photos courtesy of Wikimedia Commons

Page 104
There are enough women to do … Morahan, Shirley. *A Woman's Place: Rhetoric and Readings for Composing Yourself and Your Prose*

Now, I am all for human life … Porter, Katherine Anne. Interview, *The Paris Review Interviews, The Art of Fiction No. 29*

It is much easier, I find … Jackson, Shirley. *Come Along with Me,* from the essay "Experience and Fiction"

Page 105
A big sturdy fellow … SJLMM

Has dear, appealing ways … SJLMM

Chapter 6
Page 108
Photo of Edith Wharton courtesy of Beineke Library, Yale University, Watkins / Loomis Agency, and the estate of Edith Wharton

Page 111
Photo of LMM courtesy of Archival and Special Collections, University of Guelph Library, Guelph, Ontario, Canada

Page 112
I do not think that she ... AMOJA

She was careful that ... AMOJA
At any rate, one would ... AROO

Page 113
Sir — I have in my possession ... AMOJA

Page 114
Pen name signatures courtesy of Wikimedia Commons

Page 115
The Professor met with many ... LOCB

Drawing of Charlotte Brontë courtesy of Wikimedia Commons

Page 116
My work (a tale in one volume) ...TBTLFC

Page 117
I now send you per rail a MS .... LOCB

Page 118
Today I read an article ... SJLMM

Photo of LMM courtesy of Archival and Special Collections, University of Guelph Library, Guelph, Ontario, Canada

Page 119
I tried to write what ... Van Gelder, Robert. *Writers and Writing*, Charles Scribner's Sons, NY, 1946

Pages 121–123
I have always kept ... SJLMM

Page 122
We take pleasure in advising you ... WAL

Page 124
A Wrinkle in Time was almost ... L'Engle, Madeleine. *A Wrinkle in Time*, paperback edition

Photo of Madeleine L'Engle courtesy of Crosswicks, Ltd., in cooperation with McIntosh & Otis, Inc.

Page 126
Photo of Madeleine L'Engle and Hugh Franklin courtesy of Crosswicks, Ltd., in cooperation with McIntosh & Otis, Inc.

Page 128
May, 1868 — Mr. N wants ... LMA:HLLJ

August 26, 1868 — Proof of whole ... LMA:HLLJ

Page 129
Funny time with the publishers ... LMA:HLLJ

Page 130
Stories which editors ... distrations of a busy ... gained what I lacked ... ABG

Page 133
Photo of Virginia Woolf courtesy of the Library of Congress

Chapter 7
Page 134
Photo of LMA courtesy of New York Public Library

Page 135
Won't teach any more if ... LMA:HLLJ

Pages 136–137
Louisa May Alcott stamp, USPS, 1940

Page 137
Things look promising ... LMA:HLLJ

Page 138
People usually ask ... LMA:HLLJ

Over a hundred letters from ... SLLMA

Page 139
When I had the youth ... LMA:HLLJ

Photo of LMA courtesy of New York Public Library

Page 140
Drawing of Jane Austen courtesy of Wikimedia Commons

Page 140, continued
People are more ready ... *Illustrated Letters of Jane Austen*

I am never too busy ... I cannot help hoping that ...
LOJA

I would rather have had ... from a letter to her sister
Cassandra, multiple sources

Page 141
I was glad and proud ... TBTLFC

You do it for itself ... *The Journals of Sylvia Plath*

Drawing of Charlotte Brontë courtesy of Wikimedia
Commons

Page 142
It seems that Anne ... SJLMM

I have had a month ... SJLMM

Page 143
I received my publisher's report ... SJLMM

Last night I sat down ... SJLMM

Page 144
I don't believe in all the sorrows ... GSC

I have not a sou in ... GS–GFL

Page 145
As for me ... GS–GFL

Page 147
There is no doublt in my ... LOHBS

You ask with regard ... LOHBS

Photo of HBS Courtesy of The Harriet Beecher Stowe
Center (Hartford, CT)

Page 148
How quickly the minutes fly... EDAN

Photo of Anaïs Nin courtesy of Sky Blue Press

Page 149
I cannot make money ... From her unpublished diary,
Oct. 7, 1942, via the official Anaïs Nin Blog, Sky Blue
Press, http://anaisninblog.skybluepress.com

Page 151
Why does one write? ... McCullers, Carson. "The
Flowering Dream"

Chapter 8
Page 152
Photo of LMM courtesy of Archival and Special
Collections, University of Guelph Library, Guelph,
Ontario, Canada

Page 153
One of the reviews says ... SJLMM

Page 155
One hundred thousand copies ... LOHBS

It is wonderful that ... LOHBS

Photo of HBS courtesy of The Harriet Beecher Stowe
Center, Hartford, CT

Page 156
What will the critics of ... LOTB

To value praise or stand in awe ... TBLL

Page 157
It was said that this was ... Brontë, Charlotte.
Biographical Notice of Ellis and Acton Bell

Painting of the Brontë sisters by their brother
Branwell, courtesy of Wikimedia Commons

Page 158
I never read my reviews ... McCullers, Carson.
Illumination and Night Glare

Painting of Virginia Woolf by Roger Fry, courtesy of
Wikimedia Commons

Page 161
After things are published ... Interview with Annie
Proulx, *L.A. Times*, Oct. 18, 2008

If one has sought ... ABG

Page 162
Photos courtesy of Beineke Library, Yale University,
Watkins / Loomis Agency, and the estate of Edith
Wharton

Page 163
It is a very beautiful thought ... Dwight, Eleanor.
Edith Wharton: An Extraordinary Life

Page 164
After toiling so many years ... LMA:HLLJ

It is droll, but I can't ... *Little Women Abroad*

Page 165
I can only say to you ... SLLMA

Photo courtesy of Wikimedia Commons

Page 167
In this country a writer ... WCIP

Photo of Willa Cather courtesy of the Willa Cather
Foundation, Red Cloud, NE

Page 168
I am pestered with letters ... *My Dear Mr. M.: Letters to
G.B. MacMillan*

Photos courtesy of Wikimedia Commons

Page 169

I finished my second ... *My Dear Mr. M.: Letters to G.B.
MacMillan.*

I am now girding up ... Ibid

Page 170
I want to tell you that ... AMOJA

I must make use of this ... AMOJA

Page 171
Of course a second work ... TB:TLLFC

Grateful acknowledgment is given to the following publishers for permission to reprint copyrighted text materials:

Excerpts from *Willa Cather in Person: Interviews, Speeches, and Letters,* edited by L. Brent Bohlke, copyright © 1986, reprinted by permission of The University of Nebraska Press.

Excerpts from *A Circle of Quiet* by Madeleine L'Engle, copyright © 1972 by Madeleine L'Engle Franklin. Reprinted by permission of Farrar, Straus and Giroux, LLC.

Excerpts from *A Peculiar Treasure* and *A Kind of Magic* by Edna Ferber published by arrangement with the Edna Ferber Literary Trust.

Excerpts from *Madeleine L'Engle Herself: Reflections on a Writing Life* (Writer's Palette) by Madeleine L'Engle, copyright © 2001 by Crosswicks, Ltd. Reprinted by permission of WaterBrook Multnomah, an imprint of the Crown Publishing Group, a division of Random House, Inc.

Excerpts from *Walking on Water: Reflections on Faith and Art* by Madeleine L'Engle, copyright © 2001 by Crosswicks, Ltd. Reprinted by permission of WaterBrook Multnomah, an imprint of the Crown Publishing Group, a division of Random House, Inc.

Excerpts from *The Selected Journals of L.M. Montgomery* Volumes I – V, (© 1985, 1987, 1992, 1998, 2004, University of Guelph), edited by Mary Rubio and Elizabeth Waterston, reprinted by permission of Mary Rubio, Elizabeth Waterston, and the University of Guelph, courtesy of the L.M. Montgomery Collection, Archival and Special Collections, University of Guelph Library.

Excerpts from *The Diary of Anaïs Nin: 1966-1974* Volume VII, copyright © 1980 by Gunther Stuhlmann. Reprinted by permission of Houghton Mifflin Harcourt Publishing Co.

Excerpts from *The Early Diaries of Anaïs Nin* Volume Two, 1920-1923 copyright © 1982 by Rupert Pole as Trustee for the Anaïs Nin Trust. Reprinted by permission of Houghton Mifflin Harcourt Publishing Co.

Excerpts from *A Backward Glance* by Edith Wharton, copyright © 1934, reprinted by permission of the Edith Wharton estate and Watkins / Loomis Agency.

Excerpts from *A Room of One's Own* by Virginia Woolf, copyright © 1929 by Harcourt, Inc. and renewed 1957 by Leonard Woolf. Reprinted by permission of Houghton Mifflin Harcourt Publishing Co.

Excerpts from *A Writer's Diary* by Virginia Woolf, copyright © 1954 by Leonard Woolf and renewed 1982 by Quentin Bell and Angelica Garnett. Reprinted by permission of Houghton Mifflin Harcourt Publishing Co.

Grateful acknowledgment goes to the following for permission to reprint photographs:

Photographs of Willa Cather on pages 36, 39, 40, 93, and 167, reprinted by permission of The Willa Cather Foundation.

Photographs of Anaïs Nin on pages 18, 23, 34, and 148, reprinted by permission of Sky Blue Press.

Photographs of Madeleine L'Engle on pages 79, 94, 124, and 126, reprinted by permission, courtesy of Crosswicks, Ltd. in cooperation with McIntosh & Otis, Inc.

Photograph of Madeleine L'Engle on pages 14, 61, and the cover reprinted by permission of Wheaton College Archives & Special Collections.

Photographs of Harriet Beecher Stowe on pages 16, 26, 90, 147, and 155 and ephemera relating to Uncle Tom's Cabin on pages 26 and 147 reprinted by permission of The Harriet Beecher Stowe Center.

All photographs of L.M. Montgomery courtesy of the L.M. Montgomery Collection, Archival and Special Collections, University of Guelph Library, reprinted by permission.

All photographs of Edith Wharton, courtesy of Beineke Library, Yale University, reprinted by permission of the Edith Wharton estate and Watkins / Loomis agency.

Several friends and colleagues were instrumental to the realization of this book, and I'd like to offer my heartfelt thanks to the following:

My agent, Lisa Ekus, and Jane Falla, former literary associate at The Lisa Ekus Group, who saw enough potential in the early version of this book to encourage me to develop it, and were unwavering believers in its potential.

Sally Ekus, for her support and enthusiasm, especially when I needed a bit of cheering on.

Amy Papaelias, Assistant Professor of Design at SUNY-New Paltz, for working with me to develop a unique design for this book, no small task! As always, we made a great team.

My son, Adam Atlas, for lending his eagle eye and impeccable command of the English language at various stages of this project, and for assisting me with the mysteries of InDesign.

Authors Daphne Uviller and Victoria Moran, the former for our enjoyable and productive work sessions, and the latter for introducing me to just the right editor for this book.

Melissa Mandel, for saving me untold hours of organizing notes and biographical material.

Last, but most importantly, much gratitude goes to my editor, Mark Chimsky-Lustig, for pushing me to go further at every stage and with every detail, helping me to turn up my "voice," and lending his astute eye to the aesthetics of this book. It has been a pleasure and a privilege to work with you.

POSTAL CARD.

Thank you!

Nava Atlas is the author and illustrator of many well-known vegetarian and vegan cookbooks, including *Vegan Express, Vegan Soups and Hearty Stews for All Seasons, The Vegetarian Family Cookbook,* and *The Vegetarian 5-Ingredient Gourmet.* Her first book was *Vegetariana,* now considered a classic in its field. In addition, she has published two books of humor, *Expect the Unexpected When You're Expecting!* (a parody), and *Secret Recipes for the Modern Wife.*

Nava is also a visual artist, specializing in limited-edition artists' books and text-driven objects and installations. Her work has been shown nationally in museums, galleries, and alternative art spaces. Her limited-edition books are housed in numerous collections of artists' books, including the special collections libraries of The Museum of Modern Art (NY), National Museum of Women in the Arts (Washington, DC), National Library at the Victoria and Albert Museum (London), Brooklyn Museum, Boston Museum of Fine Arts, and dozens of academic collections.

Learn more about Nava's work at her various Web sites: VegKitchen.com, navaatlas. com, and dearliteraryladies.blogspot.com. Nava has two grown sons and lives in the Hudson Valley region of New York State with her husband.